# For Conspicuous Gallantry

## Remembering
## James Stockdale

Vice Admiral James Bond Stockdale
1923 - 2005

# For Conspicuous Gallantry

## Remembering
## James Stockdale

Jim Redman

ISBN: 978-1545147252

## DEDICATION

To the memory of a man who was an intellectual giant, an authentic hero and the supreme example of the philosopher-warrior. We are not likely to ever see his equal.

# CONTENTS

*Go tell the Spartans, stranger passing by, that here obedient to their laws we lie.*

– Greek epitaph, battle of Thermopylae

# INTRODUCTION

In Stockdale's own words:[1]

"*On September 9, 1965, I flew at 500 knots right into a flak trap, at treetop level, in a little A-4 airplane that I suddenly couldn't steer because it was on fire, its control system shot out. After ejection, I had about 30 seconds to make my last statement in freedom before I landed in the main street of a little village right ahead. And, so help me, I whispered to myself: Five years down there, at least. I'm leaving the world of technology and entering the world of Epictetus.*"

His damaged Skyhawk pitched down, then up, as every red light in the cockpit flashed and blared incessantly. As the fighter raced towards the ground, Stockdale ejected, landing in the midst of a small, hostile village. Club-wielding assailants descended upon him, beating him nearly senseless and leaving his severely damaged left leg grotesquely twisted. It was never properly set and he dragged it around without complaint for the rest of his life. The beating set the stage for the next almost 8 years of his life, most of it spent at the infamous Hoa Lo Prison, or "Hanoi Hilton."

As a prisoner of war, Stockdale was at the mercy of his North Vietnamese captors. With the help of the stoic teachings of Epictetus, he not only survived those terrible years, but managed to outwit his captors and

---

[1] Stockdale quotations herein are from his papers on Stoicism, unless otherwise noted. See chapters 6 and 7.

help his fellow inmates survive.[2]

I first met Stockdale in 1980 in Singapore. I was there at that time attending an educational conference organized by the Young Presidents Organization. Stockdale was an invited speaker. The format allowed attendees to register for lectures given by the speakers and afterward to sign up to share lunch with them along with a few other attendees. After hearing his talk I jumped at the chance to spend more time with this very remarkable, humble man. During the balance of the week long conference I sat in on repeats of his lecture, and more intimate table talk.

A few years after our first meeting, I recruited him to spend another week as a resource to a small group of San Diego YPO'ers at a retreat in Monterey, California. We were both living in the San Diego area so the connection was pretty easy to maintain.

I discovered that his story was less about the gruesome details of prison survival than it was about ethics and philosophy, especially the teachings of Stoicism. Although he valued his technical training as a Navy pilot he maintained that his grounding in the humanities was really what mattered.

After a few more contacts my admiration, respect and even fascination with his life and story continued to grow. This was an authentic hero, and more than that, an intellectual giant, a true philosopher-warrior.

A word about the narrative and duplicate passages. Excerpts from his papers on Stoicism are quoted in the

[2] Excerpted from *The Stockdale Legacy*, John Wilkins, San Diego Union-Tribune, September 2015.

x

chapters describing his capture and life as a prisoner of war, and are also found in the final two chapters. The Stoicism papers, with their emphasis on philosophical teachings, are presented here in their entirety as published by the Center for the Study of Professional Military Ethics, U.S. Naval Academy.[3]

Regarding other sources, all content and background material is freely available online and extensive use has been made of Wikipedia articles. See page 137.

Here's the rest of the memory.

Jim Redman<br>
August 2017<br>
email: jim@corpplan.com

---

[3] Approved for public release by U.S. Naval Academy, distribution unlimited.

A4E Skyhawk launch from carrier

Skyhawk attack on North Vietnam bridge

Stockdale returning from mission

The Tonkin Gulf

Prisoner

Hoa Lo prison from air

Street view

Inner courtyard

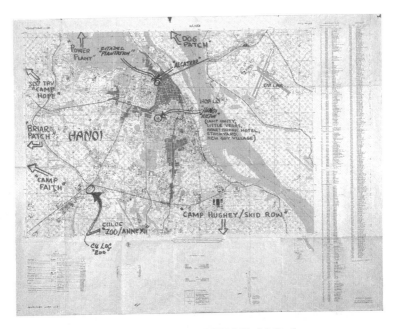

Hanoi area map by ex-POW Mike McGrath

Portrayal of POWs in leg irons

Solitary

*The returnees maintained their composure until it was clear that they were again safe under American control. No one was silent as this Air Force C-141 Starlifter left the runway at Hanoi. The photographer, TSgt Robert N. Denham, USAF, observed that "You could hear the shouts and cheers all over the aircraft" on this 28 March 1973 flight.*

Department of Defense Photo (USMC) A9000163

Released POWs safely on board US transport

Homecoming

Awarded the Medal of Honor

President of Naval War College

Memorial service at Naval Academy, 2005

# 1

## Before the War

James Bond Stockdale was born in Abingdon, Illinois on December 23, 1923, the son of Mabel Edith (nee Bond) and Vernon Beard Stockdale. His father carefully molded his young son's inner discipline and encouraged him to pursue a Navy career. After attending Monmouth College, he entered the United States Naval Academy in Annapolis, Maryland in June 1943.

On June 5, 1946 he graduated from the Naval Academy with the Class of 1947 due to the reduced schedule still in effect from World War II. Academically he ranked 130th among 821 graduates in his class. His first assignment was assistant gunnery officer aboard the destroyer minesweeper USS *Carmick* (DMS-33) from June to October 1946. He next served aboard the USS Thompson (DMS-38) from October 1946 to February

1947, the USS *Charles H. Roan* (DD-853) from February 1947 to July 1948, and the USS *Deming* (PCS-1392) from July 1948 to June 1949.

Stockdale was accepted for flight training in June 1949 and reported to Naval Air Station Pensacola in Florida. He was designated a Naval Aviator at Naval Air Station Corpus Christi in Texas, in September 1950. He was next assigned for additional training at Naval Air Station Norfolk in Virginia from October 1950 to January 1951. His piloting skills soon earned him a coveted ticket to Naval Test Pilot School at Patuxent River, Maryland. There he crossed paths with many other ambitious young fliers, including a strawberry-haired Marine named John Glenn, whom Lt. Stockdale tutored in physics and calculus. He completed his training in July 1954 and was a test pilot until January 1957. His first tour after flight training was with the VS-27, an Anti-Submarine Squadron flying Avengers.

In 1959, the U.S. Navy sent Stockdale to Stanford University where he received a master's degree in international relations and comparative Marxist thought in 1962. Initially Stockdale preferred the life of a fighter pilot over academia, but later credited Stoic philosophy with helping him cope as a prisoner of war. Like Fredrick the Great before him, Jim Stockdale was an admirer of Epictetus. He always carried a copy of the Greek philosopher's Discourses into battle with him, and these texts later proved to be an invaluable survival tool. Three years later, he returned to the sea as executive officer of the VF-51, "Flying Crusaders" and was subsequently promoted to commanding officer and deployed to the USS *Ticonderoga*. While temporarily assigned to the USS *Constellation* the squadron flew missions over Laos before returning to the *Ticonderoga*.

In his words:

*"I came to the philosophic life as a 38-year-old Navy pilot in graduate school at Stanford University. I had been in the Navy for 20 years and scarcely ever out of a cockpit. In 1962, I began my second year of studying international relations so I could become a strategic planner in the Pentagon. But my heart wasn't in it. Then I cruised into Stanford's philosophy comer one winter morning and met Philip Rhinelander, dean of humanities and sciences, who taught Philosophy 6, "The Problems of Good and Evil." Within 15 minutes, we had agreed that I would enter his two-term course in the middle. To make up for my lack of background, I would meet him for an hour a week for a private tutorial in the study of his campus home.*

*Phil Rhinelander opened my eyes. In that study, it all happened for me -- my inspiration, my dedication to the philosophic life. From then on, I was out of international relations and into philosophy. We went from Job to Socrates to Aristotle to Descartes. And then on to Kant, Hume, Dostoevsky, Camus. On my last session, he reached high on his wall of books and brought down a copy of the Enchiridion. He said, "I think you'll be interested in this."* "The time interval between my finishing graduate school and becoming a prisoner was almost exactly three years, September 1962 to September 1965. That was a very eventful period in my life. I started a war (led the first-ever American bombing raid on North Vietnam), led good men in about 150 aerial combat missions in flak, and throughout three 7-month cruises to Vietnam I had not only the Enchiridion, but the Discourses on my bedside table on each of the three aircraft carriers I flew from. And I read them."

# 2

## Captured

Stockdale led several successful strikes against North Vietnamese PT boats before witnessing the controversial episode that would bring the United States fully into the Vietnam War. On 2 August 1964, while on a DESOTO patrol in the Tonkin Gulf, the destroyer USS *Maddox* (DD-731) engaged 3 North Vietnamese Navy P-4 torpedo boats from the 135th Torpedo Squadron. After fighting a running gun and torpedo battle, in which the *Maddox* fired over 280 5-inch (130 mm) shells, and the torpedo boats expended their 6 torpedoes (all misses) and hundreds of rounds of 14.5mm machinegun fire; the combatants broke contact. As the torpedo boats turned for their North Vietnamese coastline, four F-8 Crusader fighter aircraft from USS *Ticonderoga* (CV-14) arrived, and immediately attacked the retreating torpedo boats

Stockdale (commander VF-51 (Fighter Squadron 51)), with Lieutenant (Junior Grade) Richard Hastings attacked torpedo boats *T-333* and *T-336*, while Commander R. F. Mohrhardt and Lieutenant Commander C. E. Southwick attacked torpedo boat *T-339* . The four F-8 pilots reported scoring no hits with their Zuni rockets, but reported hits on all three torpedo boats with their 20mm cannon

Two nights later, on 4 August 1964, Stockdale was overhead during the second reported attack in the Tonkin Gulf. Unlike the first event, which was an actual sea battle, no Vietnamese forces were believed to have been involved in the second engagement. In the early 1990s he recounted: "[I] had the best seat in the house to watch that event, and our destroyers were just shooting at phantom targets - there were no PT boats there . . . There was nothing there but black water and American fire power." Stockdale said his superiors ordered him to keep quiet about the details of that night.

The next morning, on 5 August 1964, President Johnson ordered bombing raids on North Vietnamese military targets which he announced were retaliation for the alleged incident of 4 August. When Stockdale was awoken in the early morning and was told he was to lead these attacks he responded: "Retaliation for what?" Later, while a prisoner of war, he was concerned that he would be forced to reveal this secret about the Vietnam War.

In his words:

*"I led all three air actions in the Tonkin Gulf affair in the first week of August 1964. Moral comers were cut in Washington in our top leaders' interpretation of the events of August 4th at sea in order to get the Tonkin Gulf Resolution through Congress in a hurry. I was not only the sole eyewitness to all events, and leader of the American forces to boot; I was cognizant of classified message traffic pertaining thereto. I knew for sure that our moral forces were squandered for short-range goals; others in the know at least suspected as much.*

*On the 9th of September 1965, I flew right into a flak trap, at tree-top level, 500 knots, in a little A-4 airplane-- cockpit walls not even three feet apart - which I couldn't steer after it was on fire, control system shot out. After ejection I had about 30 seconds to make my last statement in freedom before I landed on the main street of that little village right ahead. And so help me, I whispered to myself: "Five years down there at least. I'm leaving the world of technology and entering the world of Epictetus.*

*It's very quiet in a parachute, and I can hear the rifle shots down below and can match them up with bullet rips occurring in the parachute canopy above me. Then I can*

27

*hear the noontime shouting and see the fists waving in the town as my chute hooks a tree but deposits me on a main street in good shape. With two quick-release fastener flips, I'm free of the chute, and immediately gang-tackled by the 10 or 15 town roughnecks I had seen in my peripheral vision, pounding up the street from my right. It felt to me like the quarterback sack of the century. I don't want to make a big thing of this, nor indicate that I was surprised at my reception, but by the time the tackling and pummeling and twisting and wrenching were over, and it lasted for three or more minutes before the guy in the pith helmet got there to blow his whistle, I had a very badly broken leg that I felt sure would be with me for life. And that hunch turned out to be right."*

## Hoa Lo Prison

The name Hoa Lo, commonly translated as "fiery furnace" or even "Hell's Hole" also means "stove". The name originated from the street name Hoa Lo, due to the concentration of stores selling wood stoves and coal-fire stoves along the street from pre-colonial times. The prison was built in Hanoi by the French, in dates ranging from 1886 - 1889 and 1898 - 1901 when Vietnam was still part of French Indochina. The French called the prison *Maison Centrali*, literally Central House, a traditional euphemism to denote prisons in France. It was located near Hanoi's French Quarter and was intended to hold Vietnamese prisoners, particularly political prisoners agitating for independence who were often subject to torture and execution. A 1913 renovation expanded its capacity from 460 inmates to 600. It was nevertheless often overcrowded, holding some 730 prisoners on a given day in 1916, a figure which would rise to 895 in 1922 and 1,430 in 1933. By 1954 it held more than 2,000. With its inmates held in subhuman conditions, it had become a symbol of colonialist exploitation and of the bitterness of the Vietnamese towards the French.

The central urban location of the prison also became part of its early character. During the 1910s through 1930s, street peddlers made an occupation of passing outside messages in through the jail's windows and tossing tobacco and opium over the walls; letters and packets would be thrown out to the street in the opposite direction. Within the prison itself, communication and ideas passed. Indeed, many of the future leading figures in Communist North Vietnam spent time in Maison Centrale during the 1930s and 1940s.

During the Vietnam War, the first U.S. prisoner to be sent to Hoa Lo was Lieutenant, Junior Grade Everett Alvarez Jr., who was shot down on August 5, 1964. From the beginning, U.S. POWs endured miserable conditions, including poor food and unsanitary conditions. The prison complex was sarcastically nicknamed the "Hanoi Hilton" by the American POWs, in reference to the well-known Hilton Hotel chain. There is some disagreement among the first group of POWs over who coined the name but F8D pilot Bob Shumaker was the first to write it down, carving "Welcome to the Hanoi Hilton" on the handle of a pail to greet the arrival of Air Force Lieutenant Robert Peel.

Beginning in early 1967, a new area of the prison was opened for incoming American POWs; it was dubbed "Little Vegas", and its individual buildings and areas were named after Las Vegas Strip landmarks, such as "Golden Nugget", "Thunderbird", "Stardust", "Riviera", and the "Desert Inn." These names were chosen because many pilots had trained at Nellis Air Force Base, located in proximity to Las Vegas. American pilots were frequently already in bad shape by the time they were captured, injured either during their ejection or in landing on the ground.

The Hanoi Hilton was one of several sites used by the North Vietnamese Army to house, torture and interrogate captured servicemen, mostly American pilots shot down during bombing raids. Although North Vietnam was a signatory to the Third Geneva Convention of 1949, which demanded "decent and humane treatment" of prisoners of war, severe torture methods were employed, such as rope bindings, leg irons, beatings, and prolonged solitary confinement. When prisoners of war began to be released from this and other North Vietnamese prisons during the Johnson administration, their testimonies revealed widespread and systematic abuse of prisoners of war.

Regarding treatment at Hoa Lo and other prisons, the communists maintained that prisoners were treated well and in accordance with the Geneva Conventions. During 1969, they broadcast a series of coerced statements from American prisoners that purported to support their position. The North Vietnamese would also maintain that their prisons were no worse than prisons for POWs and political prisoners in South Vietnam, such as the one on Con Son Island. Mistreatment of Viet Cong and North Vietnamese prisoners and South Vietnamese dissidents in South Vietnam's prisons was indeed common, as was North Vietnamese treatment of South Vietnamese prisoners and their own dissidents..

Beginning in late 1969, treatment of the prisoners at Hoa Lo and other camps became less severe and generally more tolerable.

In late 1970 a rescue attempt, Operation Ivory Coast, was made at Son Tay prison camp outside Hanoi. This was a mission conducted by United States Special Operations Forces and other American military elements to rescue U.S. POWs. It was also the first joint military operation in United States history conducted under the direct control of the Chairman of the Joint Chiefs of Staff. The specially selected raiders extensively trained and rehearsed the operation at Eglin Air Force Base, Florida, while planning and intelligence gathering continued from 25 May to 20 November 1970. On 21 November 1970, a joint United States Air Force/United States Army force commanded by Air Force Brigadier General Leroy J. Manor and Army Colonel Arthur D. "Bull" Simons landed 56 U.S. Army Special Forces soldiers by helicopter in the Son Tay POW camp located only 23 miles (37 km) west of Hanoi, North Vietnam. The objective was the recovery of 61 American prisoners of war thought to be held at the camp, but the mission failed when it was found during the raid that the camp contained no prisoners. They had previously been moved to another camp. Criticism of intelligence failures, both public and within the Nixon administration, to ascertain that the camp was empty, led to a major reorganization of the United States intelligence community a year later.

After the raid most of the POWs at the outlying camps were moved to Hoa Lo, so that the North Vietnamese had fewer camps to protect. This created the "Camp Unity" communal living area at Hoa Lo, which greatly reduced the isolation of the POWs and improved their morale.

But these events were in the future. Now, it is September 9, 1965 and Commander James B. Stockdale is brought in, dragging his broken leg, and locked up for what will be almost 8 years.

# 3

## Prisoners of War

Members of the United States armed forces were held as prisoners of war (POWs) in significant numbers during the Vietnam War from 1964 to 1973. Unlike U.S. service members captured in World War II and the Korean War, who were mostly enlisted troops, the overwhelming majority of Vietnam era POWs were officers, most of them Navy, Air Force, and Marine Corps airmen; a relatively small number of Army enlisted personnel were also captured, as well as one enlisted Navy seaman who fell overboard from a naval vessel. Most U.S. prisoners were captured and held in North Vietnam by the North Vietnamese Army; a much smaller number were captured in the south and held by the National Liberation Front (Viet Cong). A handful of U.S. civilians were also held captive during the war.

As many as 13 prisons and prison camps were used to house U.S. prisoners in North Vietnam, the most widely known of which was Hoa Lo Prison (nicknamed the "Hanoi Hilton"). The treatment and ultimate fate of U.S. prisoners of war in Vietnam became a subject of widespread concern in the United States, and hundreds of thousands of Americans wore POW bracelets with the name and capture date of imprisoned U.S. service members

Stockdale was held as a prisoner of war in the Hoa Lo prison (the infamous "Hanoi Hilton") for the next seven and a half years. As the senior Naval officer, he was one of the primary organizers of prisoner resistance. Tortured routinely and denied medical attention for the severely damaged leg he suffered during capture, Stockdale created and enforced a code of conduct for all prisoners which governed torture, secret communications, and behavior.

In his words:

*"In the aftermath of the Korean War, just over 10 years before, we all had memories of reading about and seeing early television news accounts of U. S. government investigations into the behavior of some American prisoners of war in North Korea and mainland China. The gist of it was that in prison camps*

*for Americans, it was every man for himself. Since those days, I've come to know officers who were prisoners of war there, and I now see much of that as selective reporting and as a bum rap. However, there were cases of young soldiers who were confused by the times, scared to death, in cold weather, treating each other like dogs fighting over scraps, throwing each other out in the snow to die, and nobody doing anything about it.*

*This could not go on, and President Eisenhower commissioned the writing of the American Fighting Man's Code of Conduct. It was written in the form of a personal pledge. Article 4:*

If I become a prisoner of war, I will keep faith with my fellow prisoners. I will give no information or take part in any action which might be harmful to my comrades. If I am senior, I will take command. If not, I will obey the lawful orders of those appointed over me and will back them up in every way.

*In other words, as of the moment Eisenhower signed that document, American prisoners of war were never to escape the chain of command; the war goes on behind bars.*

*As an insider, I knew the whole setup; that the North Vietnamese already held about 25 prisoners, probably in Hanoi, and as I was the only wing commander to survive an ejection, that I would be their senior, their commanding officer - and would remain so, very likely, throughout this war that I felt sure would last at least another five years. And here I was, starting off crippled and flat on my back."*

In the summer of 1969, he was locked in leg irons in a bath stall and routinely tortured and beaten. When told by his captors that he was to be paraded in public, Stockdale slit his scalp with a razor to purposely disfigure himself so that his captors could not use him as propaganda. When they covered his head with a hat, he beat himself with a stool until his face was swollen beyond recognition.

In his words:

*"I put a lot of thought into what my first orders should be. They would be orders that could be obeyed, not a "cover your ass" move of reiterating some U.S. government policy like "name, rank, serial number and date of birth," which had no chance of standing up in the torture room. My mindset was, "We here under the gun are the experts, we are the masters of our fate. Ignore guilt-inducing echoes of hollow edicts, throw out the book, and write your own." My orders came out as easy-to-remember acronyms. The principal one was BACK US. Don't Bow in public; stay off the Air; admit no Crimes; never Kiss them good-bye. US could be interpreted as United States, but really meant that each of us had to work at the lowest common denominator, never negotiating for himself but only for all.*

*Prison life became a crazy mixture of an old regime and a new one. The old was the political prison routine mainly for dissenters and domestic enemies of the state. It was designed and run by old-fashioned Third-World*

*Communists of the Ho Chi Minh cut. It revolved around the idea of "repentance" for "crimes" of anti-social behavior. American prisoners, street criminals, and domestic political enemies of the state were all in the same prison. We never saw a "POW camp" like in the movies. The Communist jail was part psychiatric clinic and part reform school. North Vietnamese protocol called for making all their inmates demonstrate shame, bowing to all guards, heads low, never looking at the sky."*

## Communication

The **tap code**, sometimes called the **knock code**, is a way to encode text messages on a letter-by-letter basis in a very simple way. The message is transmitted using a series of tap sounds, hence its name. The tap code has been used by prisoners throughout history to communicate with each other. The method of communicating is usually by tapping either the metal bars, pipes or the walls inside a cell.

The tap code is based on a **Polybius square** using a 5×5 grid of letters representing all the letters of the Latin alphabet, except for K, which is represented by C. The listener only needs to discriminate the timing of the taps to isolate letters. Each letter is communicated by tapping two numbers - the first designating the row; the second designating the column. For example, to specify the letter "B", one taps once, pauses, and then taps twice. Because of the difficulty and length of time required for specifying a single letter, prisoners often devise abbreviations and acronyms for common items or phrases, such as "GN" for *Good night,* or "GBU" for *God bless you*

United States prisoners of war during the Vietnam War are known for widely using the tap code. It was introduced in June 1965 by four POWs held in the Hoa Lo "Hanoi Hilton" prison: Captain Carlyle "Smitty" Harris, Lieutenant Phillip Butler, Lieutenant Robert Peel, and Lieutenant Commander Robert Shumaker. Harris had heard of the tap code being used by prisoners in World War II and remembered a United States Air Force instructor who had discussed it as well.

In Vietnam, the tap code became a very successful way for otherwise isolated prisoners to communicate. POWs would use the tap code in order to communicate to each other between cells in a way which the guards would be unable to pick up on. They used it to communicate everything from what questions interrogators were asking (in order for everyone to stay consistent with a deceptive story), to who was hurt and needed others to donate meager food rations. It was easy to teach and newly arrived prisoners became fluent in it within a few days. It was even used when prisoners were sitting next to each other but not allowed to talk, by tapping on another's thigh. By overcoming isolation with the tap code, prisoners were able to maintain a chain of command and morale.

## Interrogation

The North Vietnamese efforts were aimed at extracting information from captives that might be useful in defense against the U.S. air strikes. But more important, they wanted to obtain "confessions" that could be released for propaganda purposes.

As Jonathan Mahler writes about Stockdale:[4]

"After a few months in solitary confinement in Hoa Lo prison in Hanoi, he was introduced to "the ropes," a torture technique in which a prisoner was seated on the floor - legs extended, arms bound behind him - as a guard stood on his back and drove his face down until his nose was mashed into the brick floor between his legs. The North Vietnamese knew they were overmatched militarily, but they figured they could at least win the propaganda war by brutalizing American P.O.W.'s until they denounced their government and

---

[4] Jonathan Mahler, *The Lives They Lived; The Prisoner*, New York Times, December 2005

"confessed" that they had bombed schoolchildren and villagers.

For his part, Stockdale intended to return home with his honor intact. One afternoon, he was given a razor and led to the bathroom -- a sure sign that he was being readied for a propaganda film. Instead of shaving, Stockdale gave himself a reverse Mohawk, tearing up his scalp in the process. More determined than ever now, his captors locked him in the interrogation room for a few minutes while they fetched a hat for him. Stockdale glanced around, looking for an appropriate weapon. He considered a rusty bucket and a windowpane before settling on a 50-pound stool, and proceeded to beat himself about the face. Then, realizing that his eyes were not yet swollen shut, he beat himself some more. By the time the guards had returned, blood was running down the front of his shirt. For the next several weeks, Stockdale kept himself unpresentable by surreptitiously bashing his face with his fists. The North Vietnamese never did manage to film him.

As Hoa Lo filled with American shootdowns, Stockdale transformed a loose colony of destabilized POWs into a tightly knit underground resistance movement with its own language (an alphabetical tap code) and laws. Stockdale was the highest-ranking Navy POW., but his authority derived less from seniority than from that rare blend of virtues that enables a small minority of men to thrive in what the Prussian military philosopher Karl von Clausewitz called the 'province of danger'.

Inside the interrogation room, the military's Code of Conduct, which presupposes adherence to the Geneva Conventions, was of little value. The torture was simply too intense to limit statements to name, rank, serial number and date of birth. So Stockdale created new rules designed both to protect America's war effort and to keep POWs alive. Stockdale ordered his men to endure as much physical abuse as they could before acceding to any of their interrogators' demands -- the key, in his view, to preserving a sense of dignity -- and to always confess to fellow inmates everything they had been forced to divulge. To carry an unclean conscience was to risk descending into a spiral of guilt and shame that would make them only more vulnerable to themselves and their captors.

Desperate as he was to return to his wife and four boys in Southern California, Stockdale was so adept at living through privation and pain that he came to feel at home inside Hoa Lo. He recalled long-forgotten details from his childhood, calculated natural logarithms with a stick in the dust and pondered the physics of musical scales. As he saw it, he was still at war, only it wasn't the Navy that had prepared him for this sort of battle, it was two ancient Greek philosophers. From Aristotle, Stockdale had learned that free will can exist within a state of imprisonment. From Epictetus, the influential Stoic, he had learned about our ability to shape experience by perception: as months of solitary confinement in leg irons and brutal beatings turned to years, Stockdale would remind himself that "men are disturbed not by things but by the view that they take of them." Most of all, he became absorbed in his battles with his captors, whether that meant planting fake notes for guards to discover or gleefully "tapping" his tales of interrogation-room intransigence to his neighbors."

In Stockdale's words:

*"In a crucible like a torture prison, you reflect, you silently study what makes those about you tick. Once I had taken the measure of my torture guard, watched his eyes as he worked, watched him move, felt him move as he stood on my slumped-over back and cinched up the ropes pulling my shoulders together, I came to know that there was good in him. That was ironic because when he first came in with the new commissar when torture was instigated after I got there, I had nicknamed him "Pigeye" because of the total vacancy of the stare of*

*the one eye he presented as he peeked through cell door peepholes. He was my age, balding and wiry, quick, lithe and strong, like an athletic trainer. He was totally emotionless, thus his emotionless eyes. He had almost no English-language capability, just motions and grunts. Under orders, he put me through the ropes 15 times over the years, and rebroke my bad leg once, I feel sure inadvertently. It was a court martial scene and he was having to give me the ropes before a board of North Vietnamese officers. The officers sat at a long table before Pigeye and me, and behind us was a semi-circle of soldiers bearing rifles with fixed bayonets at a kind of "dangle" position, the bayonet pointing at the cement floor ahead of them. This was in the "knobby" torture room of "New Guy Village" at Hoa Lo prison in August 1967 - so-called because the walls had been crudely speckled with blobs of cement the size of an ice cream scoop in a "soundproofing" attempt. I could tell Pigeye was nervous because of these officers whom I had never seen before, and I don't think he had, and he pressed me flat over my bad leg instead of the good one he had always put the tension on before. The healing knee cartilage gave way with a loud "pop," and the officers looked at each other and then got up and left. I couldn't get off that floor and onto my feet for nearly two months.*

*In all those years, we probably had no more than 24 hours, one-on-one together. But neither of us ever broke the code of an unvaryingly strict "line of duty" relationship. He never tricked me, always played it straight, and I begged no mercy. I admired that in him, and I could tell he did in me. And when people say: "He was a torturer, didn't you hate him?" I say, like Solzehnitsyn, to the astonishment of those about me, "No, he was a good soldier, never overstepped his line of duty."*

Stockdale was also instrumental in bringing about the end of prisoner torture, but it nearly cost him his life. He was charged with starting a prison riot and an officer told him before leaving him for the night, "Tommorrow Sto-dale we will bring you down." Stockdale was made to sit up in a chair all night in leg irons and ropes on his arms. He learned that Ho Chi Minh had died the night before on Sept. 3rd, 1969. North Vietnam was unstable due to the death of its icon, and Stockdale made this work to his advantage. During the night, he slashed his wrists with a piece of broken glass. The guards discovered him near death and revived him. Stockdale's actions convinced his captors he was prepared to die rather than give in. The beatings stopped and the torture-happy prison commander was replaced.

## Alcatraz Gang

Stockdale was one of eleven prisoners known as the "Alcatraz Gang": George Coker; George McKnight;

Jeremiah Denton; Harry Jenkins; Sam Johnson; James Mulligan; Howard Rutledge; Robert Shumaker; Ronald Storz; and Nels Tanner. These individuals had been leaders of resistance activities while in captivity and thus were separated from other captives and placed in solitary confinement. "Alcatraz" was a special facility in a courtyard behind the North Vietnamese Ministry of National Defense, located about one mile away from Hoa Lo Prison. In Alcatraz, each of the prisoners was kept in an individual windowless concrete cell measuring 3 by 9 feet (0.91 by 2.74 m) with a light bulb kept on around the clock, and they were locked in leg irons each night. Storz died in captivity there in 1970.

These 11 prisoners of war were separated because they were leaders of the prisoners' resistance led by Stockdale. Of Stockdale, Coker said "He was the strongest, most exemplary leader of the whole North Vietnamese POW environment." Coker and McKnight were the last POWs assigned to the Alcatraz Gang, being so assigned for previous fierce resistance to their treatment and an unsuccessful escape from the Power Plant or "Dirty Bird" prison camp. The POWs considered some things as just "mistreatment" not real torture, such as their ankles being shackled to the floor. Torture was being hung from the ceiling by ropes.

The group received special torture and were taken into torture sessions in order of rank, highest to lowest.

Coker was the youngest and lowest ranking of the eleven POWs and was taken in last. He said he is still grateful for every minute the others held out. During the end of his session, something changed and the session stopped, which the POWs thought was because of a political decision from higher authorities to stop the sessions. All of the prisoners except Storz were moved to other prisons in December 1969. Storz, debilitated from sickness and untreated injuries, was left behind and died in captivity on 23 April 1970.

In the end, North Vietnamese torture was sufficiently brutal and prolonged that virtually every American POW so subjected made a statement of some kind at some time. As one later wrote of finally being forced to make an anti-American statement: "I had learned what we all learned over there: Every man has his breaking point. I had reached mine." Realizing this, the Americans' aim became to absorb as much torture as they could before giving in. One later described the internal code the POWs developed, and instructed new arrivals on, as: "Take physical torture until you are right at the edge of losing your ability to be rational. At that point, lie, do, or say whatever you must do to survive. But you first must take physical torture"

After making statements, the POWs would admit to each other what had happened, lest shame or guilt consume them or make them more vulnerable to additional

FOR CONSPICUOUS GALLANTRY

North Vietnamese pressure. Nevertheless, the POWs obsessed over what they had done, and would years after their release still be haunted by the "confessions" or other statements they had made. As another POW later said, "To this day I get angry with myself. But we did the best we could. [We realize], over time, that we all fall short of what we aspire to be. And that is where forgiveness comes in."

The North Vietnamese occasionally released prisoners for propaganda or other purposes. The POWs had a "first in, first out" interpretation of the Code of the U.S. Fighting Force, meaning they could only accept release in the order they had been captured but making an exception for those seriously sick or badly injured. When a few captured servicemen began to be released from North Vietnamese prisons during the Johnson administration, their testimonies revealed widespread and systematic abuse of prisoners of war. Initially, this information was downplayed by American authorities for fear that conditions might worsen for those remaining in North Vietnamese custody. Policy changed under the Nixon administration, when mistreatment of the prisoners was publicized by U.S. Secretary of Defense Melvin Laird and others, especially Sybil Stockdale.

Beginning in October 1969, the torture regime suddenly abated to a great extent, and life for the prisoners became less severe and generally more tolerable. North Vietnamese leader Ho Chi Minh had died the previous month, possibly causing a change in policy towards POWs. Many POWs speculated that Ho had been personally responsible for their mistreatment. Also, a badly beaten and weakened POW who had been released that summer disclosed to the world press the conditions to which they were being subjected, and the efforts of Sybil Stockdale and the National League of Families of American Prisoners and Missing in Southeast Asia heightened awareness of the POWs' plight.

By 1971, some 30-50 percent of the POWs had become disillusioned about the war, both because of the apparent lack of military progress and what they heard of the growing anti-war movement in the U.S., and some of them were less reluctant to make propaganda statements for the North Vietnamese. Others were not among them; there were defiant church services and an effort to write letters home that only portrayed the prison in a negative light. Such prisoners were sometimes sent to a camp reserved for "bad attitude" cases.

At the "Hanoi Hilton", POWs cheered the resumed bombing of North Vietnam starting in April 1972, whose targets included the Hanoi area. The old-time POWs cheered even more during the intense "Christmas Bombing" campaign of December 1972 when Hanoi was subjected for the first time to repeated B-52 Stratofortress raids. Although the explosions lit the night sky and shook the walls of the camp, rattling some of the newer POWs, most saw it as an effective measure to compel North Vietnam to finally come to terms.

American POWs in North Vietnam were released in early 1973 as part of Operation Homecoming, the result of diplomatic negotiations concluding U.S. military involvement in Vietnam. On February 12, 1973, the first of 591 U.S. prisoners began to be repatriated, and return flights continued until late March. After Operation Homecoming, the U.S. still listed roughly 1,350 Americans as prisoners of war or missing in action and sought the return of roughly 1,200 Americans reported killed in action but whose bodies were not recovered. These missing personnel would become the subject of the long running Vietnam War POW/MIA issue.

## George Coker

*The following gripping account of one prisoner's personal experience is by Joanne Kimberlin, writing for* The Virginian-Pilot:[5]

"If you're never tested, you don't know," says George Coker.

Coker has been tested. Shot down over North

---

[5] Joanne Kimberlin, *Locked Up For 6 Years, He Unlocked A Spirit Inside,* The Virginian-Pilot, Nov 11, 2008

Vietnam, he spent 6½ years in captivity. Most of it was hard time - the kind they make movies about, the kind only a fanatical enemy can deliver.

Today, Coker is the head of a state organization of POWs, as well as a Hampton Roads chapter. Time has pushed him to the front of the room. Men who walked tall through earlier wars now shuffle into the group's monthly get-togethers.

Coker shepherds the meetings, as well as the men. Lately he's been urging them to get their burial benefits in order; too many have died without taking care of things. And he nags the men to write down their stories while they still can.

"Individually they're fascinating," Coker says, "but collectively - wow."

He drags his feet when it comes to his own story. His wife, Pam, keeps after him, mostly so his descendants will someday know. But Coker hesitates, unsure he can do it justice with a pen.

"People ask, 'What was it like?' Six and half years. You can't answer that question in two sentences."

Aug. 27, 1966, was supposed to be a "milk run. " Coker was on his 30th mission in the cockpit of an A-6A Intruder, zooming over jade-colored hills in the panhandle of North Vietnam. He and pilot

Jack Fellowes were zeroing in on a bridge they were assigned to destroy.

Without warning, the jet snapped crazily. A wing had been blown in half. Coker still isn't sure by what. "A lucky shot," he says.

Not for the men in the jet. There was nothing to do but eject. Coker's arm and knee were torn up punching through the canopy. When he floated to the ground , "20 of them were waiting for me with open arms. "

He was stripped of his flight gear, arms tied behind his back.

"I'd lost a lot of blood. I was pretty much in a state of shock."

For the next few days, "I was roughed up, slapped around. They were trying to get some information. I could dodge most of it by pretending to be young and stupid. I didn't tell them anything that wasn't on my clipboard or on my gear ."

Fellowes was captured about three miles from Coker.

"We didn't see each other for about four days," Coker says. "Then they started trucking us north. We were blindfolded most of the time. Jack and I managed to realize both of us were there. We didn't talk much. There wasn't a lot to talk about.

My injuries were getting infected by then, and I was getting in pretty bad shape."

The ride was made longer by some of Coker's own work.

"It took an entire day to find some reconstructed bridge to get us into Hanoi, " he says with a touch of pride. "We had taken out a lot of their transportation."

He and Fellowes were thrown into Hoa Lo Prison. Sarcastically nicknamed the "Hanoi Hilton," the compound would later hold John McCain, though he and Coker did not come face to face until after the war. "We called it 'HBH,'" "Coker says, "or Heartbreak Hotel.'" At first, it wasn't so bad.

"It was my luck - other people's misfortune - that they were really working over some senior officers who had been shot down, so I was at the bottom of the barrel. It gave me some time to figure out what was going on. Build up your gumption. Get ready for the inevitable."

He was moved to a place the men called "the Zoo," on the outskirts of the city. His knee was seriously infected by now, a fever that ran up and down his leg. Interrogations were getting tougher . In late September, after fists had failed to persuade him, Coker began what he describes as "probably my worst experience in Vietnam" - "the wall."

Each morning, a gong sounded at 5:30. Coker got up in his cell and stood facing the wall, hands above his head. He stayed there until another gong rang at 10 p.m. About two weeks into it, his knee began oozing black. One night he was hauled off to a hospital. He was afraid they were going to cut off his leg. It was still there when he woke up from the chloroform. Incisions had been made to drain the infection.

"Temporarily that was good. It kept me off the wall for two whole days. On the third day, somebody came in and said, 'What the hell's wrong with you? Get up against the wall!' The sabbatical was over."

"The wall" went on for more than two months. "That's a real long story," Coker says. "A hard, emotional story. I don't know if I'm going to tell it all the way through."

In essence: "It becomes a mental fight. Why are you doing this? Don't do it. I quit. If they see you, they could come in and beat the crap out of you. That's instant pain - that's not particularly comfortable. A lot of it is just not giving in, not wanting to give in - for spite, if nothing else - refusing to yield." Principles drilled into Coker long ago by coaches and Scout leaders helped shore him up. He could picture the banner that hung in his Catholic high school, Benedict, in New Jersey.

"'Benedict's hates a quitter.' I heard it said many, many times." To occupy his mind, Coker built houses in his head, nail by nail.

"One for the lake, one for the ocean, one for cliffs, one for the beaches, one for flat stuff, you name it." He designed cars, took trips, laid out menus. "That's just one tiny little aspect of what you did....Except slowly, my mind couldn't function. It was slowing down, kind of like you were almost mentally dying."

The things that kept him going:

"Family, but it got to the point where I couldn't remember my family. I didn't know their names. I couldn't say them." And religion:

"That 's a very, very powerful thing. I remember saying rote prayers. It got to a point I couldn't say a prayer." For some reason, Scouting stayed with him. He doesn't know why.

"The last thing I was hanging on to was the Boy Scout oath....I could only get through the first sentence or so: 'On my honor, I'll do my best...' Those were the only words I could focus in my brain.... I'd long since forgotten my family names,

God, country, everything else."

Two days before Christmas 1966: "They came in and said, 'You don't have to get up against the wall anymore.' I just collapsed. I woke up about two days later."

Five months after being captured, Coker finally had company. He was moved to "Little Vegas" - a new compound specially built at the Hanoi Hilton. With few common walls, it was designed to foil the prisoners' tapping code. Coker shared an 8-foot-by-8-foot cell with three Air Force guys. "At least I had somebody to talk to."

Tapping continued, using the floor or what shared walls existed. "It didn't take long to get in trouble." Communication leads to organization, which breeds resistance. The jailers were determined to put a stop to it.

"Starting in early July, they went on a real purge. They wanted to know who was doing what, who you were talking to. And they started to torture people really hard. My turn came at the end of August."

Coker has given the definition of torture a lot of thought in the years since. Some of today's interrogation methods - such as waterboarding - might qualify in his book. Tactics that embarrassed the United States at Iraq's Abu

Ghraib prison do not.

"If they had threatened me that I was going to have to have women take pictures of me in my skivvies, I'd have said, 'Go at it, pal.... That's OK by me.' I'm not trying to defend it, but you've got to realize there's a humongous difference between that and somebody who's really being brutalized. We had an understanding amongst ourselves of what hard-core torture really was."

A few days in stocks were viewed as mere "mistreatment." Iron cuffs were bolted to the floor and locked around the ankles. Prisoners could lie down flat or sit up straight, but they could not twist or turn.

"That becomes pretty uncomfortable if you've got to stay in stocks a day or so or if they don't let you out at all or - topping it off - if they handcuff your hands behind your back.... If it goes on about a week, you're being tortured."

"The ropes" were torture in everyone's eyes. Upper arms were tied behind the back until the elbows touched . They were then pulled up over the prisoner's head. At times, the rope was run through a hook in the ceiling and the prisoner lifted off the ground until his own weight pulled his arms out of joint.

Such obvious, long-term injuries made the

interrogators nervous, though. "They knew that someday they might have to pay for that."

They resorted to tying prisoners into a ball. Arms were still cinched behind the back, only now the leverage came from passing the rope over the prisoner's shoulder and tying it to his ankles. "Not only were your shoulders aching like crazy, now that's putting pressure on your hips. Every joint in your body is screaming in agonizing pain. Most people can't take that 10, 15 minutes - half an hour at the most.... It hurts so much you got to do something. But when you do something, it doesn't have to be useful or truthful. That's a hard lesson to learn. Sometimes you figure once you break a little bit, you've broken totally."

Soon afterwards, Coker tried to escape. He'd been taken to a compound that was less secure. He and another prisoner, George McKnight, whittled away at the locks on their cells, slipped past the guards at night, shimmied along pipes, crossed the roof and climbed over a wall.

They made it to the river, tied themselves together and let its current carry them downstream, past the junks and sampans of Hanoi, into the countryside. "At one point, George looked at me and said, 'Someday this is going to be a great story to tell your grandkids.' I said, 'Right. First we've got to live long enough to have kids, much less grandkids.' "

They were discovered the next morning hiding in a hole along the riverbank. "The Great Escape was over after about 12 hours." It earned Coker a beating that ruptured his eardrums and a ticket to the prison known as "Alcatraz."

Ringleaders of POW resistance were banished to Alcatraz. Among those already there: Jeremiah Denton, who would later become an admiral and a U.S. senator, and James Stockdale, commanding officer of all POWs, future Medal of Honor winner and vice-presidential candidate.

"There were 11 of us. Four have since died. The rest of us remain extremely close . We had a very unique experience, even among the Vietnam group. It was the best of comradeship and the worst of living conditions."

Each man was in solitary. Coker spent two years alone in a 9-foot-by-3-foot cell under a light bulb that burned 24 hours a day. Each night, a guard came in to lock him in irons. The men fortified each other with tapping.

Occasionally, Coker would catch a glimpse of the others - a pair of eyes watching through a cell door slit as he was led down the hall for more "sessions."

Interrogations had a new goal now. The North Vietnamese wanted propaganda - statements from the prisoners that condemned the US and its involvement in the war. They aimed to sway international opinion in their favor and erode support back in America for the war.

"We decided, 'No, we're not going to cooperate with it,'" Coker says. "Every guy had to take maximum torture before he'd write anything." Senior ranks were taken in first.

"As the junior guy," Coker says, "this was really bad. They'd be out for two or three weeks. Beaten. Ropes. All this time, I'm watching, and I'm in a total state of terror before they even open the door."

Finally, they came for him. At one point during the next week, he was left alone in a room with a desk. He pulled out a drawer and used it to pound his right hand until it was broken. When his captors returned, they informed him that he would simply write with his left.

He tried to give them enough to make it stop.

"When you couldn't take anymore, you'd write down something about the government and throw all this other stuff in to make sure anybody else would realize it's bogus trash. You could tell the way they came in the next day if they were happy or not. Mine must have been really bad. That's when I got the fan-belt beating."

Stripped naked, on the floor, 50 lashes, from shoulders to calves. Tomorrow, he was told, there would be 100.

"For whatever reason, I just decided I wasn't going to do it. They came back that afternoon and I said no. They said, 'You have a very, very bad attitude, and we will determine what we're going to do with you.'

"That was weird. Something had changed within a 12-hour period. We knew there was a big political battle going on. Apparently, word came down saying 'no more.' "

If the punishment had gone on much longer, Coker doesn't know what might have been. He's grateful to the men who went before him - for every minute they held out. They bought him the time that ran out in the end.

"You often wonder what's worth it. And it's hard for me to tell those guys - even at the time."

Coker was taken out of Alcatraz on Dec. 9, 1969. For the next three years, he bounced between prisons. There was talk that the war might end soon. For the most part, things got better. Hard core torture stopped. Food improved. Long-term solitary was rare.

He used the time to get better.

"We were wacko cases when we came out of Alcatraz. I didn't realize how bad I was and how much damage had been done psychologically." Now surrounded by other prisoners, he retreated to a corner and soaked it in.

"I just loved listening to these guys. They'd tell stories, they'd tell about movies, talk about their families. I just sat and listened, and I thought it was grand."

Coker got out on March 4, 1973, in one of four waves of prisoner releases that year . So much had changed in his absence - seven years of unprecedented social upheaval. Sex, drugs and rock 'n' roll.

"All those things happened in that very tumultuous period, and we weren't here at all. We were strangers in our own country, and we didn't like a lot of what we saw."

To a great extent, Coker says, Vietnam vets "stepped back. We didn't understand, so we didn't accept it. For 30 years, we just kept quiet. In a way, we've lived a separate psychological life because we had a totally different experience because we were gone."

Three decades have helped the POWs of Vietnam blend back in. Their ordeal, however, remains a part of who they are.

Joints still throb from the ropes. Many of the men wrestle with post-traumatic stress disorder. Coker's wife Pam sometimes sees it when her husband goes to bed. He mumbles, sweats, tosses and turns. She has noticed his hands above his head.

"In his sleep, he holds up 'the wall,' " she says.

Coker chooses not to dwell on it. In the face of such brutality, he saw the best of the human spirit.

"You're capable of a great deal more than you realize, if you really set your mind to it. Look at me. I did it, and there's nothing special about me. I'm just another guy ... just like those World War II guys or in Korea or me in Vietnam or these guys right now, you can do a tremendous amount."

Part of that, Coker says, requires "realizing there's something better or bigger than just yourself. That was real for us. We don't want to be preachy about it, but I hope the message gets through."

## The Stockdale Paradox[6]

*From an interview between author James C. Collins and Stockdale at Stanford after the war:*

"You can understand, then, my anticipation at the prospect of spending part of an afternoon with Stockdale. One of my students had written his paper on Stockdale, who happened to be a senior research fellow studying the Stoic philosophers at the Hoover Institution right across the street from my office, and Stockdale invited the two of us for lunch. In preparation, I read *In Love and War*, the book Stockdale and his wife had written in alternating chapters, chronicling their experiences during those eight years.

As I moved through the book, I found myself getting depressed. It just seemed so bleak - the uncertainty of his fate, the brutality of his captors, and so forth. And then, it dawned on me: "Here I am sitting in my warm and comfortable office, looking out over the

---

[6] Excerpted from James C. Collins, *Good to Great*

beautiful Stanford campus on a beautiful Saturday afternoon. I'm getting depressed reading this, and I know the end of the story! I know that he gets out, reunites with his family, becomes a national hero, and gets to spend the later years of his life studying philosophy on this same beautiful campus. If it feels depressing for me, how on earth did he deal with it when he was actually there and *did not know the end of the story?*

"I never lost faith in the end of the story," he said, when I asked him. "I never doubted not only that I would get out, but also that I would prevail in the end and turn the experience into the defining event of my life, which, in retrospect, I would not trade."

I didn't say anything for many minutes, and we continued the slow walk toward the faculty club, Stockdale limping and arc-swinging his stiff leg that had never fully recovered from repeated torture. Finally, after about a hundred meters of silence, I asked, "Who didn't make it out?"

"Oh, that's easy," he said. "The optimists."

"The optimists? I don't understand," I said, now completely confused, given what he'd said a hundred meters earlier.

"The optimists. Oh, they were the ones who said, 'We're going to be out by Christmas.' And Christmas would come, and Christmas would go. Then they'd say, 'We're going to be out by Easter. And Easter would come, and Easter would go. And then Thanksgiving, and then it would be Christmas again. And they died of a broken heart."

Another long pause, and more walking. Then he turned to me and said,

"This is a very important lesson. You must never confuse faith that you will prevail in the end - which you can never afford to lose - with the discipline to confront the most brutal facts of your current reality, *whatever they might be.*"

To this day, I carry a mental image of Stockdale admonishing the optimists: "We're not getting out by Christmas; *deal with it.*"

# 4

## Remembering Sybil[7]

"Sybil Stockdale was a Navy officer's wife, trained not to rock the boat. Then her husband, a fighter pilot, was shot down over North Vietnam in September 1965.

The boat got rocked.

Mrs. Stockdale, whose death was announced Tuesday by the Navy, defied a government "code of silence" about the POWs and went public in 1968. That prompted American authorities to openly criticize the North Vietnamese, who in turned stopped mistreating the prisoners.

---

[7] Excerpted from POW Wife Dies, John Wilkins, San Diego Union-Tribune, October 15, 2015.

Early in Stockdale's captivity, his wife, Sybil Stockdale, organized The League of American Families of POWs and MIAs, with other wives of servicemen who were in similar circumstances. By 1968, she and her organization, which called for the President and the U.S. Congress to publicly acknowledge the mistreatment of the POWs (something that had never been done despite evidence of gross mistreatment), gained the attention of the American press. Sybil Stockdale personally made these demands known at the Paris Peace Talks.

"In an era when women weren't typically looked to as leaders, Sybil Stockdale was one of the most extraordinary leaders during one of the most difficult times in American history," said Alvin Townley, author of "Defiant," a 2014 book about the POWs. "She helped launch a movement that united a terribly divided nation around a common goal: Bringing home our prisoners of war."

Mrs. Stockdale, a longtime Coronado resident, died Saturday, according to the Navy. She was diagnosed with Parkinson's Disease several years ago. She would have turned 91 next month.

She and her husband, James Stockdale, had been married for 18 years and had four sons when his A-4 Skyhawk was shot down on a bombing mission. He disappeared into a hellhole of torture and deprivation the prisoners dubbed the "Hanoi Hilton."

Stockdale's leadership there -- creating secret ways to communicate, establishing a code of conduct, smashing his face and cutting his scalp to prevent his captors from using him in a propaganda film -- rallied the other prisoners, many of whom credited him with saving their lives. After the war, Stockdale was awarded the Medal of Honor.

He always said his wife was the courageous one.

In Coronado, in between taking care of the family and working as a school teacher, she began organizing informal gatherings of POW/MIA wives and other relatives, a group that eventually became the National League of Families. Mrs. Stockdale was its first national coordinator, traveling often to Washington, D.C., to meet with government officials.

"She was our hero, our leader, our everything," said Shirley Stark of Coronado, whose husband, Bill, was shot down in May 1967. At first, the group heeded the government's request not to say anything about the POWs, lest their words undermine ongoing negotiations about the war. But quietly, Mrs. Stockdale seethed. She couldn't understand why officials listed her husband as "missing" when she'd received prison letters from him. And it was clear to her from those letters, from the language he used and from his penmanship, that he was being mistreated.

Finally, in October 1968, she went public in an interview in the San Diego Union. "The North Vietnamese have shown the only thing they care about is world opinion," she said.

Other media picked up the story, other wives began speaking out, and by the time President Richard M. Nixon took office the following January, he had thousands of telegrams on his desk urging him to do something about the POWs.

"It was not a well-known issue until Sybil Stockdale and the other wives made it an issue," Townley said. "They realized that if they didn't make it an issue, the government was going to forget about their husbands.

"In May 1969, Nixon's defense secretary, Melvin Laird, held a news conference accusing the North Vietnamese of violating the Geneva Convention. The torture soon stopped.

"She was proud when it all came to fruition and the administration changed its tune and acknowledged that the POWs were being brutally treated," her son Sid Stockdale said. "She really felt validated by that, and by the way the public embraced the prisoners."

In addition to her public advocacy, Mrs. Stockdale was taught by intelligence officers how to share secret messages with her husband -- some hidden behind photos that peeled away when soaked in liquid, others written on invisible carbon paper -- so that information could be passed back and forth.

For her actions, Mrs. Stockdale was given the Navy's Distinguished Public Service Award, the only wife of an active-duty naval officer ever to receive that honor. The citation accompanying the award credits her "indomitable spirit in the face of many adversities."

"In February 1973, after the United States agreed to a cease-fire, James Stockdale and almost 600 other POWs came home. When his plane landed at Miramar Naval Air Station, he knew his wife would be waiting on the tarmac. His vision and hearing were damaged, he had a severe limp and he couldn't raise one of his arms, but he told himself, "Stand up straight now. You've got to make her proud."

He retired from the Navy in 1978 and moved into academia, serving as president at the Citadel and as a research fellow at Stanford's Hoover

Institution. In 1984, he and his wife co-authored a memoir, "In Love and War," about their Vietnam ordeal. It became a TV movie three years later starring James Woods and Jane Alexander.

"It's still one of those core books for young Navy wives," Sid Stockdale said.

Vice Adm. Stockdale died in 2005. A guided missile destroyer is named after him, as are annual leadership awards in the Pacific and Atlantic fleets. There is an exhibit that honors both Stockdales at the NTC Command Center at Liberty Station.

Even when they lived elsewhere, the Stockdales kept their home in Coronado, where she hosted monthly reunions of local POW families, including one about 10 days ago. "We were making plans for her birthday party next month," Stark said. "People were going to come in from all over." Last month, she attended the opening reception for a new exhibit at the Coronado Historical Association called "Stockdale: Character, Community, Leadership."

Born Sybil Elizabeth Bailey, she grew up in East Haven, Conn., where her father and uncle operated a dairy. She graduated from Mount Holyoke College and was teaching at a private girls' school in Richmond, Va., when she met her future husband, a midshipman at the Naval Academy, on a blind date in 1946. They were married a year later.

Life as a Navy wife meant a lot of moves over the years -- more than 30 in all, including one in 1957 to Palo Alto, where she got a master's degree in education at Stanford. By 1995, they had settled full-time in Coronado.

Mrs. Stockdale is survived by three sons, Jim Stockdale of Beaver, Pa., Sid Stockdale of Albuquerque, N.M., and Taylor Stockdale of Claremont, along with their wives and eight grandchildren. In addition to her husband, she was preceded in death by another son, Stanford.

Sybil Stockdale was buried beside her husband on the grounds of the U.S. Naval Academy in Annapolis, Maryland."

REMEMBERING JAMES STOCKDALE

.

# 5

## After the War

Not long after he was finally released in early 1973, Stockdale said he had no intention of becoming a professional ex-P.O.W., yet his 2,714 days in captivity powerfully shaped the rest of his life. Stockdale drifted professionally - not like the stereotypically disillusioned Vietnam vet, but in nevertheless unmistakable ways. He was given different peacetime commands, all of which felt like comedowns from his service in Vietnam, both as a commander and as an underground prison boss. "In those jobs under life-and-death pressure, what I said, what I did, what I thought, really had an effect on the state of affairs of my world," he would later reflect.

Stockdale retired from the Navy in 1979 to become president of the Citadel, a civilian military college in South Carolina, but quit a year later when the board blocked his efforts to rein in the school's out-of-control culture of hazing. ("When you've been tortured by professionals, you do not have to put up with amateurs," he told a friend, explaining his abrupt decision to resign.)

Then came Stockdale's ill-fated foray into politics. His friend Ross Perot had assured him that he would be only a placeholder until he could find a suitable running mate for the 1992 presidential election -- a couple of weeks, Perot told him. Stockdale had spent longer blindfolded, naked on the floor, with an untreated broken leg in his cell in Vietnam. He figured he could get through this fine.

He didn't. After delivering the unforgettable opening line in the vice presidential debate -- "Who am I? Why am I here?" -- Stockdale was reduced to a national laughingstock. Even then there was a whiff of tragedy, a sense that he deserved better, but he disappeared from the public stage before much more could be said about him. He was last seen by many Americans in the person of Phil Hartman on "Saturday Night Live."

The former fighter pilot found solace in the world of ideas. He was inevitably pulled back to Hoa Lo, and to a better understanding of the qualities that enable certain men to stand up and turn their world around -- "the rising of the few," as he called it. For guidance, Stockdale turned to the writings of other ex-prisoners: Viktor Frankl, Aleksandr Solzhenitsyn, Fyodor Dostoyevsky. Stockdale gradually came to see heroism not as a matter of consistent good judgment but as a single act, or series of acts, performed in a particular context. And he came to see heroes not as people who had carried out their duty with distinction but as individuals who had, like himself, done something no reasonable person would ever have felt justified asking them to do.

Over the course of his 37 year military career, Stockdale had become a hero to countless American soldiers and citizens, while earning 26 personal combat decorations in the process, including the Medal of Honor, for his courage and leadership at the Hoa Lo POW prison.

The quiet academic life seemed to suit Stockdale and in 1981 he became a senior research fellow at the Hoover Institute, at Stanford University.

He died on July 5, 2005, at his home near San Diego, California and is buried at the U.S. Naval Academy, Annapolis, Maryland.

# Medal of Honor Citation

"FOR CONSPICUOUS GALLANTRY *and intrepidity at the risk of his life above and beyond the call of duty while senior naval officer in the Prisoner of War camps of North Vietnam. Recognized by his captors as the leader in the Prisoners' of War resistance to interrogation and in their refusal to participate in propaganda exploitation, Rear Adm. Stockdale was singled out for interrogation and attendant torture after he was detected in a covert communications attempt. Sensing the start of another purge, and aware that his earlier efforts at self-disfiguration to dissuade his captors from exploiting him for propaganda purposes had resulted in cruel and agonizing punishment, Rear Adm. Stockdale resolved to make himself a symbol of resistance regardless of personal sacrifice. He deliberately inflicted a near-mortal wound to his person in order to convince his captors of his willingness to give up his life rather than capitulate. He was subsequently discovered and revived by the North Vietnamese who, convinced of his indomitable spirit, abated in their employment of excessive harassment and torture toward all of the Prisoners of War. By his heroic action, at great peril to himself, he earned the everlasting gratitude of his fellow prisoners and of his country. Rear Adm. Stockdale's valiant leadership and extraordinary courage in a hostile environment sustain and enhance the finest traditions of the U.S. Naval Service.*"

Congressional Medal of Honor

# 6

## Master of My Fate[8]

"When I debated Al Gore and Dan Quayle on television in October 1992, as candidates for vice president, I began my remarks with two questions that are perennially debated by every thinking human being: Who am I? Why am I here? The questions were relevant in terms of the evening's purpose, which was to introduce myself and let the American people know where I was coming from. But I also chose them for their broader relevance to my life: I am a philosopher.

I came to the philosophic life as a 38-year-old Navy pilot in graduate school at Stanford University. I had been in the Navy for 20 years and scarcely ever out of a cockpit. In 1962, I began my second year of studying international relations so I could become a strategic planner in the Pentagon. But my heart wasn't in it. Then I cruised into Stanford's philosophy corner one winter morning and met Philip Rhinelander, dean of

---

[8] From *Stockdale on Stoicism*, one of two papers published by Center for the Study of Professional Military Ethics, U.S. Naval Academy.

humanities and sciences, who taught Philosophy 6, "The Problems of Good and Evil." Within 15 minutes, we had agreed that I would enter his two-term course in the middle. To make up for my lack of background, I would meet him for an hour a week for a private tutorial in the study of his campus home.

Phil Rhinelander opened my eyes. In that study, it all happened for me -- my inspiration, my dedication to the philosophic life. From then on, I was out of international relations and into philosophy. We went from Job to Socrates to Aristotle to Descartes. And then on to Kant, Hume, Dostoevsky, Camus. On my last session, he reached high on his wall of books and brought down a copy of the *Enchiridion*. He said, "I think you'll be interested in this."

## Epictetus and the *Enchiridion*

*Enchiridion* means "ready at hand." In other words, it is a handbook. Its author, Epictetus, was a very unusual man of intelligence and sensitivity who gleaned wisdom rather than bitterness from his early first-hand exposure to extreme cruelty, the abuse of power, and self-indulgent debauchery.

Epictetus was born a slave around 50 A.D. At 15 he was sold at a slave auction in Rome to Epaphroditus, a secretary to Emperor Nero. When Epaphroditus helped Nero complete his suicide attempt, Epictetus was able to venture out on his own.

Being a serious and doubtless disgusted young man, he gravitated to the high-minded public lectures of the Stoic teachers who were then the philosophers of Rome. Epictetus eventually became apprenticed to the very best Stoic in the empire, Musonius Rufus. After ten or more years of study, he achieved the status of philosopher in his own right. With that came true freedom, and the preciousness of that was duly celebrated by the former slave. In his works, individual freedom is praised about seven times more frequently than it is in the New Testament. The Stoics held that all human beings were equal in the eyes of God: male and female, black and white, slave and free.

Epictetus speaks like a modem person, using "living speech," not the literary Attic Greek we are used to in men of that tongue. The *Enchiridion* was actually penned not by Epictetus, who was above all else a determined teacher and man of modesty who would never take the time to transcribe his own lectures, but by one of his most meticulous and determined students, Arrian, who, with Epictetus's consent, took down his words verbatim. Arrian bound the lectures into books; in the two years that he was enrolled in Epictetus's school, he filled eight books. Arrian put the *Enchiridion* together as highlighted extractions "for the busy man." That last morning, Rhinelander told me, "As a military man, I think you'll have special interest in this. Frederick the Great never went on a campaign without a copy of this hand-book in his kit."

Stoicism is a noble philosophy that has proven to be more practicable than a modem cynic would expect. The Stoic viewpoint is often misunderstood because the casual reader misses the point - that all talk is in reference to the "inner life." Stoics belittle physical harm, but this is not braggadocio. They are speaking of it in comparison to the devastating agony of shame they fancied good men generating when they knew in their hearts that they had failed to do their duty *vis-à-vis* their fellow men or God. Though pagan, the Stoics had a monotheistic natural religion and were great contributors to Christian thought. The fatherhood of god and the brotherhood of man were Stoic concepts prior to Christianity. In fact, Chrysippus, one of their early theoreticians, made the analogy of what might be called the soul of the universe to the breath of a human (*pneuma*, in Greek). Saint Paul, a Hellenized Jew brought up in Tarsus, a Stoic town in Asia Minor, always used the Greek work *pneuma*, or breath, for soul.

The Stoic demand for disciplined thought naturally won only a small minority to its standard, but those few were the strongest characters of that time. In theory a doctrine of pitiless perfectionism, Stoicism actually created men of courage, saintliness, and goodwill. Rhinelander singled out three examples: Cato the Younger, Emperor Marcus Aurelius, and Epictetus. Cato was the great Roman Republican who pitted himself against Julius Caesar. He was the unmistakable hero of our own George Washington; scholars find quotations of Cato in Washington's Farewell Address - without quotation marks. Emperor Marcus Aurelius took the Roman Empire to the pinnacle of its power and influence. And Epictetus, the great teacher, played his part in changing the leadership of Rome from the swill he had known under Nero to the power and decency it knew under Marcus Aurelius.

Epictetus drew the same sort of audience Socrates had drawn 500 years earlier - young aristocrats destined for careers in finance, the arts, public service. The best families sent him their sons in their middle 20s - to be told what the good life consisted of, to be disabused of the idea that they deserved to become playboys, and to be taught that their job was to serve their fellow men.

Epictetus explained that his curriculum was not about *"revenues or income, or peace or war, but about happiness and unhappiness, success and failure, slavery and freedom."* His model graduate was not a person *"able to speak fluently about philosophic principles as an idle babbler, but about things that will do you good if your child dies, or your brother dies, or if you must die or be tortured... Let others practice lawsuits, others study problems, others syllogisms; here you practice how to die, how to be enchained, how to be racked, how to be exiled."* A man is responsible for his own *"judgments, even in dreams, in drunkenness, and in melancholy madness."* Each individual brings about his own good and his own evil, his good fortune, his ill fortune, his happiness, and his wretchedness. It is unthinkable that one man's error could cause another's suffering; suffering, like everything else in Stoicism, was all internal - remorse at destroying yourself.

Epictetus was telling his students that there can be no such thing as being the "victim" of another. You can only be a "victim" of yourself. It's all in how you discipline your mind. Who is your master? "He who has authority over any of the things on which you have set your heart....What is the result at which all virtue aims? Serenity....Show me a man who though sick is happy, who though in danger is happy, who though in prison is happy, and I'll show you a Stoic.

## Fighter Squadron Commander

When I got my degree, Sybil and I packed up our four

sons and family belongings and headed to Southern California. Our new home was to be in Coronado. I was to take command of fighter squadron 51, flying supersonic F-8 Crusaders, at Miramar and at sea aboard carriers. Exactly three years after we drove out of our driveway in Los Altos Hills, I was shot down and captured.

I was not a bookworm throughout those three years before I was shot down; most of the time I was busy at sea in the western Pacific. I launched on three seven-month cruises, all centered on the buildup and explosions of the Southeast Asian war. I was in command throughout, the last cruise as the commander of the air wing on the *Oriskany*. I dropped the first bombs of the war into North Vietnam and flew more than 100 missions in the flak.

But I was a changed and better man for my introduction to philosophy, and especially to Epictetus. I was on a different track - certainly not an anti-military track, but to some extent an anti-organization track. Against the backdrop of all the posturing and fumbling that peacetime military organizations seem to have to go through, to accept the need for graceful and unselfconscious improvisation under pressure, to break away from set procedures, forces you to be reflective as you put a new mode of operation together. I had become a man detached - not aloof but detached - able to throw out the book without the slightest hesitation when it no longer matched the external circumstances. I was able to put juniors over seniors without embarrassment when their wartime instincts were more reliable. This new abandon, this new built-in flexibility I had gained, was to pay off later in prison.

My bedside table on the ship was stacked not with

busywork to impress my boss, but with Stoic readings: the *Discourses,* Xenophon's *Memorabilia,* recollections of Socrates, and of course, *The Iliad* and *The Odyssey.* Epictetus expected his students to be familiar with Homer's plots.

The Stoics were the ultimate warriors. The Roman Stoics coined the formula, *Vivere Militare! -* Life is being a soldier. Epictetus said in *Discourses: "Do you not know that life is a soldier's service? One must keep guard, another go out to reconnoiter, another take the field. If you neglect your responsibilities when some severe order is laid upon you, do you not understand to what a pitiful state you bring the army in so far as in your lies?"*

Enchiridion: *"Remember, you are an actor in a drama of such sort as the Author chooses - if short, then in a short one; if long, then in a long one. If it be his pleasure that you should enact a poor man, or a cripple, or a ruler, see that you act it well. For this is your business - to act well the given part, but to choose it belongs to Another...Every one of us, slave or free, has come into this world with innate conceptions as to good and bad, noble and shameful, becoming and unbecoming, happiness and unhappiness, fitting and inappropriate...If you regard yourself as a man and as a part of some whole, it is fitting for you now to be sick and now to make a voyage and run risks, and not to be in want, and on occasion to die before your time. Why, then, are you vexed? Would you have someone else be sick of a fever now, someone else go on a voyage, someone else die? For it is impossible in such a body as ours, that is, in this universe that envelopes us, among these fellow creatures of ours, that such things should not happen, some to one man, some to another."*

## Becoming a Prisoner

On September 9, 1965, I flew at 500 knots right into a flak trap, at treetop level, in a little A-4 airplane that I suddenly couldn't steer because it was on fire, its control system shot out. After ejection, I had about 30 seconds to make my last statement in freedom before I landed in the main street of a little village right ahead. And, so help me, I whispered to myself: "Five years down there, at least. I'm leaving the world of technology and entering the world of Epictetus."

"Ready at hand" from the *Enchiridion* as I ejected from that airplane was the understanding that a Stoic always kept separate files in his mind for those things that are "up to him" and those things that are "not up to him." Another way of saying it is those things which are "within his power" and those things which are "beyond his power." Up to me, within my power, within my will, are my opinions, my aims, my aversions, my own grief, my own joy, my attitude about what is going on, my own good, and my own evil.

To explain why "your own good and your own evil" is on that list, I quote Alexander Solzehnitsyn's *Gulag Archipelago: "Gradually it was disclosed to me that the line separating good and evil passes not between states nor between classes nor between political parties, but right through every human heart."* Long before reading Solzehnitsyn, I learned that good and evil are not abstractions - the only good and evil that mean anything are right in your own heart.

But a greater realization is that of your own fragility; that you could be reduced as I was from leading over 100 pilots and 1,000 men to "taking the ropes" in a matter of minutes. This is an example of not having control over your station in life.

Everybody does have to play the game of life. You can't just walk around saying, "I don't give a damn about health, or wealth, or whether I'm sent to prison or not." Epictetus says everybody should play the game of life - that the best play it with "skill, form, speed, and grace." But like most games, you play it with a ball. Your team devotes all its energies to getting the ball across the line. But after the game, what do you do with the ball? Nobody much cares. It's not worth anything. The competition, the game, was the thing. The ball was "used" to make the game possible, but it in itself is not of any value that would justify falling on your sword for it.

The ball-game analogy, incidentally, is almost a verbatim quote of Epictetus's explanation to his students in Necropolis, colonial Greece, 2,000 years ago.

## My Mission in Prison

So I took those core thoughts into prison; I also remembered a lot of attitude shaping remarks. Here's Epictetus on how to stay off the hook: *"A man's master is he who is able to confer or remove whatever that man seeks or shuns. Whoever then would be free, let him wish nothing, let him decline nothing, which depends on others; else he must necessarily be a slave."* And here's why never to beg: *"For it is better to die of hunger, exempt from fear and guilt, than to live in affluence and with perturbation."* Begging sets up a demand for *quid pro quo,* deals, agreements, reprisals - the pits.

If you want to protect yourself from "fear and guilt" - and those are the crucial pincers, the real long term destroyers of will - you have to get rid of all your instincts to compromise, to meet people halfway. You have to learn to stand aloof, never give openings for deals, never level with your adversaries. You have to become what Ivan Denisovich called a "slow movin' cagey prisoner."

All that, over the previous three years, I had unknowingly put away for the future. So when bailing out of my A-4, after the gang tackling and pummeling was over (it lasted for two or three minutes before a man with a pith helmet got there to blow his police whistle), I had a very badly broken leg that I felt sure would be with me for life. My hunch turned out to be right. Later, I felt some relief - but only minor - from another admonition of Epictetus that I remembered: *"Lameness is an impediment to the leg, but not to the Will; and say this to yourself with regard to everything that happens. For you will find such things to be an impediment to something else, but not truly to yourself."*

So in prison I had become a man with a mission. To explain this, let me unload a little emotional baggage that was part of my military generation's legacy in 1965.

In the aftermath of the Korean War, just over 10 years before, we all had memories of reading about and seeing early television news accounts of U. S. government investigations into the behavior of some American prisoners of war in North Korea and mainland China. The gist of it was that in prison camps for Americans, it was every man for himself. Since those days, I've come to know officers who were prisoners of war there, and I now see much of that as selective reporting and as a bum rap. However, there were cases of young soldiers who were confused by the times, scared to death, in cold weather, treating each other like dogs fighting over scraps, throwing each other out in the snow to die, and nobody doing anything about it.

This could not go on, and President Eisenhower commissioned the writing of the American Fighting Man's Code of Conduct. It was written in the form of a personal pledge. Article 4:

*If I become a prisoner of war, I will keep faith with my fellow prisoners. I will give no information or take part in any action which might be harmful to my comrades. If I am senior, I will take command. If not, I will obey the lawful orders of those appointed over me and will back them up in every way.*

In other words, as of the moment Eisenhower signed that document, American prisoners of war were never to escape the chain of command; the war goes on behind bars.

As an insider, I knew the whole setup; that the North Vietnamese already held about 25 prisoners, probably in Hanoi, and as I was the only wing commander to survive an ejection, that I would be their senior, their commanding officer - and would remain so, very likely, throughout this war that I felt sure would last at least another five years. And here I was, starting off crippled and flat on my back.

Epictetus turned out to be right. All told, it was only a temporary setback from things that were important to me, and being cast in the role as the sovereign head of an American expatriate colony which was destined to remain autonomous, out of communication with Washington, for years on end, was very important to me. I was determined to "play well the given part."

The key word for all of us at first was fragility. Each of us, before we were ever in shouting distance of another American, was made to "take the ropes." That was a real shock to our systems - and as with all shocks, its impact on our inner selves was a lot more impressive and lasting and important than to our limbs and torsos. These were the sessions where we were taken down to submission and made to blurt out distasteful confessions of guilt and American complicity into antique tape recorders, and then to be put in what I call "cold soak," six or eight weeks of total isolation to "contemplate our crimes." What we actually contemplated was what even the most self-satisfied American saw as his betrayal of himself and everything he stood for. It was there that I learned what "Stoic harm" meant. A shoulder broken, a bone in my back broken, and a leg broken twice were peanuts by comparison. Epictetus said: *"Look not for any greater harm than this: destroying the trustworthy, self-respecting, well-behaved man within you."*

When put into a regular cell block, hardly an American came out of that without responding something like this when first whispered to by a fellow prisoner next door: "You don't want to talk to me; I am a traitor." And because we were equally fragile, it seemed to catch on that we all replied something like this: "Listen, pal, there are no virgins in here. You should have heard the kind of statement I made. Snap out of it. We're all in this together. What's your name? Tell me about yourself." To hear that last was, for most new prisoners just out of initial shake-down and cold soak, a turning point in their lives.

## A Society of Prisoners

We organized a clandestine society via our wall tap code - a society with our own laws, traditions, customs, even heroes. To explain how it could be that we would order each other into more torture, order each other to refuse to comply with specific demands, intentionally call the bluff of our jailers and force them to repeat the process described above, I'll explain with an apocryphal statement that could have come from at least half of those wonderful, competitive fly-boys I found myself locked up with:

*"We are in a spot like we've never been in before. But we deserve to maintain our self-respect, to have the feeling we are fighting back. We can't refuse to do every degrading thing they demand of us, but it's up to you, boss, to pick out things we must all refuse to do, unless and until they put us through the ropes again. We deserve to sleep at night. We at least deserve to have the satisfaction that we are hewing to our leader's orders. Give us the list: What are we to take torture for?"*

This was a first step in claiming what was rightfully ours. Epictetus said: "The judge will do some things to you which are thought to be terrifying; but how can he

95

stop you from taking the punishment he threatened?" That's my kind of Stoicism. You have a right to make them hurt you, and they don't like to do it. The prison commissar told my fellow prisoner Ed Alvarez when he was released: "You Americans were nothing like the French; we could count on them to be reasonable."

I put a lot of thought into what my first orders should be. They would be orders that could be obeyed, not a "cover your ass" move of reiterating some U.S. government policy like "name, rank, serial number and date of birth," which had no chance of standing up in the torture room. My mindset was, "We here under the gun are the experts, we are the masters of our fate. Ignore guilt-inducing echoes of hollow edicts, throw out the book, and write your own." My orders came out as easy-to-remember acronyms. The principal one was BACK US. Don't **B**ow in public; stay off the **A**ir; admit no **C**rimes; never **K**iss them good-bye. **US** could be interpreted as United States, but really meant that each of us had to work at the lowest common denominator, never negotiating for himself but only for all.

Prison life became a crazy mixture of an old regime and a new one. The old was the political prison routine mainly for dissenters and domestic enemies of the state. It was designed and run by old-fashioned Third-World Communists of the Ho Chi Minh cut. It revolved around the idea of "repentance" for "crimes" of anti-social behavior. American prisoners, street criminals, and domestic political enemies of the state were all in the same prison. We never saw a "POW camp" like in the movies. The Communist jail was part psychiatric clinic and part reform school. North Vietnamese protocol called for making all their inmates demonstrate shame, bowing to all guards, heads low, never looking at the sky. It meant frequent sessions with your interrogator, if for no other reason than to check your attitude. And if judged "wrong," then you were maybe down the torture chute of confession of guilt, of apology, and then the inevitable payoff - the atonement.

The new regime, superimposed on the above, was for Americans only. It was a propaganda factory, supervised by young, English speaking, bureaucratic army officers with quotas to fill, quotas set by the political arm of the government: press interviews with visiting left-wing Americans, propaganda films to shoot (starring intimidated people they called "American Air Pirates"), and so on.

An encapsulated history of how this bifurcated prison philosophy fared is this: The propaganda footage and interviews started to backfire. Smart American college men were salting their acts with double-meaning sentences, gestures read as funny-obscene by Western audiences, and practical jokes. One of my best friends, tortured to give names of pilots he knew who had turned in their wings in opposition to the war, said there were only two: Lieutenants Clark Kent and Ben Casey. That went on the front page of the *San Diego Union,* and somebody sent a copy back to the government in Hanoi. As a result of that friendly gesture from a fellow American, Nels Tanner went into three successive days of rope torture, followed by 123 days in leg stocks - all while isolated, of course.

So after several of these stunts, which cost the Vietnamese much loss of face, North Vietnam resorted to getting its propaganda from only the relatively few Americans they could trust not to act up - real loners who, for different reasons, never joined the prisoner organization, never wanted to get into the tap-code network, well known sleaze balls we came to call "finks."

The great mass of the other Americans in Hanoi were, by all standards, "honorable prisoners," but that is not to say that there was anything like a homogeneous prison regime we all shared. People like to think that because we were all in the Hanoi prison system, we had all these common experiences. It's not so. These differing regimes became marked when our prison organization stultified the propaganda efforts of this two-headed monster called the "Prison Authority." The North Vietnamese turned to vengeance against the leadership of my organization and to an effort to break down the morale of the others baiting them with an amnesty program in which they would compete for early release by being compliant to North Vietnam's wishes.

## To the Dark Place

In May 1967, the PA system blared out: "Those of you who repent, truly repent, will be able to go home before the war is over. Those few diehards who insist on inciting the other criminals to oppose the camp authority will be sent to a special dark place." I immediately put out an order forbidding any Americans to accept early release, but that is not to say I was a lone man on a white horse. My order was accepted with obvious relief and spontaneous jubilation by the overwhelming majority.

Guess who went to the dark place. They isolated my leadership team - myself and my ten top cohorts - and sent us into exile. The Vietnamese worked very hard to learn our habits, and they knew who were the trouble makers and who were not making any waves. They isolated those I trusted most: those with a long record of solitary and rope-mark pedigrees. Not all were seniors. One of my 10 was only 24 years old - born after I was in the Navy. He was a product of my recent shipboard tendencies: "When instincts and rank are out of phase, take the guy with the instincts." All of us stayed in solitary throughout, starting with two years in leg irons in a little high-security prison right beside North Vietnam's "Pentagon" - their Ministry of Defense, a typical, old French building.

There are chapters upon chapters after that, but what they came down to in my case was a strung out vengeance fight between the Prison Authority and those of us who refused to quit trying to be our brothers' keepers. The stakes grew to nervous-breakdown proportions. One of the 11 of us died in that little prison we called Alcatraz. There was not a man who wound up with less than three and a half years of solitary, and four of us had more than four years.

Howie Rutledge, one of the four of us with more than four years, went back to school and got a master's degree after we got home. His thesis concentrated on the question of whether long-term erosion of human purpose was more effectively achieved by torture or isolation. He mailed out questionnaires to us (who had also taken the ropes at least 10 times), and others with records of extreme prison abuse. He found that those who had less than two years' isolation and plenty of torture said torture was the trump card; those with more than two years' isolation and plenty of torture said that, for long term modification of behavior, isolation was the way to go. From my viewpoint, you can get used to repeated rope torture - there are some tricks for minimizing your losses in that game. But keep a man, even a very strong willed man, in isolation for three or more years, and he starts looking for a friend, any friend, regardless of nationality or ideology.

Epictetus once gave a lecture to his faculty complaining about the common tendency of new teachers to slight the stark realism of Stoicism's challenges in favor of giving the students an uplifting, rosy picture of how they could meet the harsh requirements of the good life painlessly. Epictetus said: *"Men, the lecture room of the philosopher is a hospital; students ought not to walk out of it in pleasure, but in pain."* If Epictetus's lecture room was a hospital, my prison was a laboratory - a laboratory of human behavior. I chose to test his postulates against the demanding real life challenges of my laboratory.

I'm not talking about brainwashing; there is no such thing. I'm talking about having looked over the brink, and seen the bottom of the pit, and realizing the truth of that linchpin of Stoic thought: that the thing that brings down a man is not pain but shame!

Why did those men in "cold soak" after their first rope trip eat their hearts out and feel so unworthy when the first American contacted them? Epictetus knew human nature well. In that prison laboratory, I know of not a single case where a man was able to erase his pangs of conscience with some laid back, pop-psychology theory of cause and effect. Epictetus emphasizes time and again the fact that a man who lays the causes of his actions onto third parties or forces is not leveling with himself. He must live with his own judgments if he is to be honest with himself. "But if a person subjects me to fear of death, he compels me," says a student. "No," says Epictetus, *"It is neither death, nor exile, nor toil, nor any such things that is the cause of your doing, or not doing, anything, but only your opinions and the decisions of your Will."*

"What is the fruit of your doctrines?" someone asked Epictetus. *"Tranquility, fearlessness, and freedom,"* he answered. You can have these only if you are honest and take responsibility for your own actions. You've got to get it straight! You are in charge of you.

In prison, I never tapped or mentioned Stoicism once. You soon learned that if the guy next door was doing okay, that meant that he had all his philosophical ducks lined up in his own way. But some sharp guys read the signs in my actions. After one of my long isolations outside the cell blocks of the prison, I was brought back into signaling range of the fold. My point of contact was a man named Dave Hatcher. As was standard operating procedure on a first contact after a long separation, we started off not with gushes of news but with, first, an agreed-upon danger signal; second, a cover story for each of us if we were caught; and third, a back-up communications system if this link was compromised - "slow movin' cagey prisoner" precautions. Hatcher's backup system for me was a note drop by an old sink near a place we called the Mint, the isolation cell-block of this wing of the prison - a place he rightly guessed I would soon enough be in. Every day we would signal for 15 minutes, over a wall between his cell-block and my "no-man's-land."

## Try to Check Out

Then I got back into trouble. At that time, the commissar of prisons had had me isolated and under almost constant surveillance for the year since I had staged a riot in Alcatraz to get us out of leg irons. I was barred from all prisoner cell blocks. I had special handlers, and they caught me with an outbound note that gave leads I knew the interrogators could develop through torture. The result would be to implicate my friends in "black activities," as the North Vietnamese called them. I had been through those ropes more than a dozen times, and I knew I could contain material - so long as they didn't know I knew it. But this note would open doors that could lead to more people getting killed in there. We had lost a few in big purges - I think in torture overshoots - and I was getting tired of it.

It was the fall of 1969. I had been in this role for four years, and saw nothing left for me to do but check out. I was solo in the main torture room in an isolated part of the prison the night before what they told me would be my day to spill my guts. There was an eerie mood in the prison. Ho Chi Minh had just died and special dirge music was in the air. I was to sit up all night in traveling irons. My chair was near the only pane-glass window in the prison.

I was able to waddle over and break the window stealthily. I went after my wrist arteries with the big shards. I had knocked the light out, but the patrol guard happened to find me passed out in a pool of blood but still breathing. The Vietnamese went to General Quarters, got their doctor, and saved me.

Why? It was not until after I was released years later that I learned that that very week, my wife, Sybil, was in Paris demanding humane treatment for prisoners. She was on world news, a public figure, and the last thing the North Vietnamese needed was me dead. There was a very solemn crowd of senior North Vietnamese officers in that room as I was revived. Prison torture, as we had known it in Hanoi, ended for everybody that night.

Of course, it was months before we could be sure that was so. All I knew at the time was that, in the morning, after my arms had been dressed and bandaged, the commissar himself brought in a hot cup of sweet tea, told my surveillance guard to take off my leg irons, and asked me to sit at the table with him. "Why did you do this, Sto-dale? You know I sit with the army's General Staff; they've asked for a full report this morning." (It was not unusual for us to talk like that by that time.) But he never once mentioned the note, nor did anybody else thereafter. That was unprecedented. After a couple of months in a tiny isolated cell we called Calcutta to let my arms heal, they blindfolded me and walked me right into the "Las Vegas" cell block. The isolation and special surveillance were over. I was put, solo of course, in the Mint.

Dave Hatcher knew I was back because I walked under his window, and though he could not peek out, he could listen, and over the years he had attuned his ear to my walking "signature," my limping gait. Soon enough, the rusty wire over the sink in the washroom was bent to the north - Dave Hatcher's signal for "note in the bottle under the sink for Stockdale." Like an old fighter pilot, I checked my six o'clock, scooped the note up fast, and concealed it in my prison pajama pants, carefully. Back in my cell, after the guard locked the door, I sat on my toilet bucket - where I could stealthily jettison the note if the peephole cover moved - and unfolded  Hatcher's sheet of low-grade paper toweling on which he had printed with rat dropping, without comment or signature, the last verse of Ernest Henley's poem *Invictus:*"

*It matters not how straight the gate,*
*How charged with punishment the scroll, I am the*
*master of my fate:*
*I am the captain of my soul.*

# 7

## Stoic Warrior's Triad[9]

"I feel at home here. I've flown combat with Marines in their own air planes - VMF212 out of Kaneohe. I was Wing commander of the carrier *Oriskany* on its 1965 cruise. One of our Fighter Squadrons was transitioning from F8 Crusaders to F4s. The gap was filled by the Marine F8 squadron.

The skipper was Lieutenant Colonel Chuck Ludden, the Executive Officer was Major Ed Rutty, former Blue Angel. And my wingman in the squadron was a First Lieutenant named Duane Wills (later a Lieutenant General and head of Marine Corps Aviation). I spent 7½ years in prison with my shipmate Marine Captain Harley Chapman, who was shot down two months after I was. So I'm in familiar territory, and damned glad to have spent 37 years in the Naval Service with the likes of guys like you.

Now, that said, I've got to choose my words well and get to the point if we are to get anything out of this

---

[9] Lecture to Marine Corp Warfare School, April 18, 1995, later published as one of two papers on *Stockdale on Stoicism*, by the Center for the Study of Professional Military Ethics, U.S. Naval Academy.

morning. We're going to take some big steps right away. What kind of a racket *is* this military officership? Let's go right to the old master, Clausewitz. He said: "War is an act of violence to compel the enemy to do your will." *Your* will, not *his* will. We are in the business of breaking people's wills. That's all there is to war; once you have done that, the war is over.

And what is the most important weapon in breaking people's wills? This may surprise you, but I am convinced that holding the moral high ground is more important than firepower. For Clausewitz, war was not an activity governed by scientific laws, but a clash of *wills*, of *moral forces.* He wrote: "It is not the loss in men, horses, or guns, but in order, courage, confidence, cohesion and plan which come into consideration whether the engagement can still be continued; it is principally the *moral forces* which decide here." *Moral forces! Conviction! Mind games!*

I had the wisdom of Clausewitz' stand on moral integrity demonstrated to me throughout a losing war as I sat on the sidelines in a Hanoi prison. To take a nation to war on the basis of any provocation that bears the smell of fraud is to risk losing national leadership's commitment when the going gets tough. When our soldiers' bodies start coming home in high numbers, and reverses in the field are discouraging, a guilty conscience in a top leader can become the Achilles heel of a whole country. Men of shame who know our road to war was not cricket. are seldom those we can count on to hold fast, stay the course.

As some of you know, I led all three air actions in the Tonkin Gulf affair in the first week of August 1964. Moral corners were cut in Washington in our top leaders' interpretation of the events of August 4$^{th}$ at sea in order to get the Tonkin Gulf Resolution through Congress in a hurry. I was not only the sole eyewitness to all events, and leader of the American forces to boot; I was cognizant of classified message traffic pertaining thereto. I knew for sure that our moral forces were squandered for short-range goals; others in the know at least suspected as much.

Mind games are important, and you have to play them honestly and seriously in this business. Clausewitz' battlefield enemy Napoleon not only agreed with his adversary, he made the same point of ethics in even more vivid terms.

Napoleon said: "In war, the moral is to the physical as three is to one."

I'm going to concentrate on a *major* mind game today: Stoicism. Its seeds were planted in fourth century (B.C.) Athens, as a backlash against Plato's preoccupation with inuring everybody to the perfect society. Diogenes of Sinope, a friend of both Aristotle and Alexander the Great, (they all knew each other and all died within a two-year period), struck out on *his* campaign, not to conquer the East as did Alexander, not to stamp out ignorance as did Aristotle, but to do something about *man's* condition as a cowed citizen of a city state, without anything to believe in that could defuse the inner *fears and desires* which continually obsessed him. Man had to take command of his *inner self,* control himself. *The Stoic goal was not the good society, but the good man!*

And a lot of movements sprang up, mainly in the East, after the premature crumbling of Alexander the Great's empire in Asia after his early death; dozens of cults designed to improve men's *souls* organized themselves and headed West from Athens - among others Epicureans, of course the Stoics, and finally, almost bringing up the rear, the Christians.

To get my message today, you have only to have a general understanding of the message of one man: the Stoic philosopher Epictetus, *the* outstanding pagan moralist of the Roman Empire. I'll do my best to give you that understanding in a couple of 50-minute talks with a break in between. And for the remaining time, mainly through questions and answers, we'll discuss the worthiness of what I'll call Epictetus's *"Code of Conduct'* to be part of us as warriors. Code of Conduct? You thought Stoicism was a whole philosophy with a certain cosmology, a unique logic, a physics, a theory of knowledge, and all the rest? If so, you are right, it has all the accoutrements of a philosophy; it's just that Old Man Epictetus ignored everything about it except what it had to say about personal *conduct,* how the good *man* should *think,* and *behave.* "What do I care," Epictetus asked, "whether all existing things are composed of atoms, or of indivisibles, or of fire and earth? Is it not enough to learn the true nature of the *good and the evil?"*

The first principle of Stoicism is to live in harmony with nature - human nature and physical nature. My geneticist friend at Harvard, E. O. Wilson, tells me that the difference between men and animals is not reason, but human nature. Human nature is mostly genetically driven passions, passions designed to give us the capacity to survive and reproduce. It was David Hume who said, "Reason not only *is* but *ought to be* the slave of passions." *Physical* nature, the other half, is the physical universe and all its interactions. To the Stoic, physical nature is God's body. Have a look at yourself and see where you fit into the natural scheme of things. And play the part well.

Epictetus was impatient with unmanliness and loose living. He had a sarcasm that stripped affection bare. He had a fiery earnestness, which robbed his rude strokes of their cruelty. His message: "A man must think hard and live simply to do well."

I met old Epictetus back in graduate school in 1962. It was my great luck; in fact, it was a fluke that put us together. My favorite (philosophy) professor gave me one of Epictetus's books as a farewell present as I left to go back to sea. He had never mentioned him in class. Phil Rhinelander just thought Epictetus and I would make a good pair, and he was certainly right. I had never heard of Epictetus; in fact, today his name recognition is in about the third tier of philosophers. But his mind is *first tier*.

Everything I know about Epictetus I've developed *myself* over the years. It's been a one-on-one relationship. He's been in combat with me, leg irons with me, spent month-long stretches in blindfolds with me, has been in the ropes with me, has taught me that my *true business* is maintaining control over my moral purpose, in fact that my moral purpose *is* who I am. He taught me that I am totally responsible for everything I do and say; and that it is I who decides on and controls my own destruction and own deliverance. Not even God will intercede if He sees me throwing my life away. He wants me to be autonomous. He put *me* in charge of *me*. "It matters not how straight the gate, how charged with punishment the scroll. I am the master of my fate, I am the captain of my soul."

Don't be disturbed about my occasional references to the way the Stoics see God. He's the closest thing to the Christian God there is, according to Paul Tillich, a renowned Protestant theologian. Epictetus had heard of

Christians, but he never knew any, nor were the Christians and the Stoics in competition in his lifetime. It was not until the latter part of the second century A.D. that a coherent Christian creed was beginning to emerge. Before that, nobody could state a cause *for* Christianity that would be intelligible to the pagan intellectual. The Stoics practiced a monotheistic religion from which Christianity borrowed much - the fatherhood of God and the brotherhood of man were well-established Stoic concepts before Christ was born; the Holy Ghost was a Stoic idea before Christ was born.

A quick thumbnail sketch of Epictetus's life goes like this: He was born to a Greek-speaking slave woman in a little town in Asia Minor, up in the hills behind Ephesus about a hundred miles. At the time he was born, 50 A.D., that part of the world was a Roman colony with garrisoned troops. His mother's town, Hieopolos, was then and still is renowned for its natural hot springs and baths, and I think of it as probably an R and R spot for Roman troops. (I've visited there, of course.) Born to a slave, Epictetus was automatically a slave; he had a tough life. Crippled by a cruel master, he had a bad leg just like mine - left leg at the knee. When he was about 15, he was chained up and carried away in a slave caravan bound for Rome. He was bought at auction by a former slave, a "freedman" named Epaphroditus, secretary to the Emperor of Rome, the young (27-year-old) squirt Nero. Nero was bad and getting worse by the time young Epictetus moved into the Roman "White House." By the time Nero was 30, he had killed his half brother, his first wife, second wife, and mother. And he was letting the Empire run itself. The Roman Senate declared him a public enemy, and Epaphroditus was at Nero's side as the army was breaking down the door to arrest the Emperor. Nero tried to cut his own throat, muffed it, and Epaphroditus finished the job. Epaphroditus forever thereafter lived under a cloud, and Epictetus just took to the streets of Rome. A high-minded, intelligent, Greek-speaking, young man, he started attending philosophy lectures given in the public parks. And in those days in Rome, "philosophy" was synonymous with Stoicism.

The turning point in his life was his adoption by Musonius Rufus, the very best teacher of philosophy in first-century Rome. Though Epictetus was still technically a slave, Rufus, an Etruscan knight, took him as a student. Rufus was as fluent in Greek as he was in Latin, and he and Epictetus got on well. In one passage, Epictetus tells of his tutor's mastery of seminar instruction: *"Rufus spoke in such a way that each of us, as we sat there, fancied someone had gone to him and told him of our faults; so effective was his grasp of what men actually do and think. So vividly did he set before each man's eyes his particular weakness."*

Epictetus's tutelage ran on for at least 10 years, and then Rufus launched him on a career as a bonafide philosopher of Rome. Epictetus, like all philosophers in Rome, was exiled by Emperor Domitian in the year 89 A.D., and he picked out a little town of Nicopolis (where I've also been), on the Adriatic coast of Greece, as a place to found a school. My favorite authorities set the date of his death at 138 A.D., at age 88. I've come across nothing about his "retirement," so I think of him as starting his school in about 90 A.D. at age 40, and teaching there for another 40 or 50 years. This little book like the one I got from my professor in 1962 is called *The Enchiridion*, meaning in Greek "ready at hand." It is only selected excerpts from eight volumes of Epictetus's lectures and conversations given, we think, in the year 108 A.D. He was talking to basically rich, young men from formidable families, mostly from Athens and Rome. It was the Socrates scene all over again, 500 years later - the same students, same age, mid-20s, the same type of dialogue.

Epictetus, a bachelor until his very late years when he took a wife his age to help him care for an infant he rescued from death by "exposure," was a "natural," extraordinarily gifted teacher. He was gregarious - never missed the Olympic games which were conducted only about 50 miles from his school. He talks about the Olympics of those years in *Enchiridion*:

*In every affair, consider what precedes and what follows, and then undertake it. Otherwise you will begin with spirit, indeed, careless of the consequences, and when these are developed, you will shamefully desist. I would conquer at the Olympic Games. But consider what precedes and what follows, and then, if it be for your advantage, engage in the affair. You must conform to rules, submit to a diet, refrain from dainties; exercise your body, whether you choose it or not, at a stated hour, in heat and cold; you must drink no cold water, and sometimes no wine. In a word, you must give yourself up to your trainer as to a physician. Then, in the combat, you may be thrown into a ditch, dislocate your arm, turn your ankle, swallow an abundance of dust, receive stripes [for negligence], and after all, lose the victory. When you have reckoned up all this, if your inclination still holds, set about the combat.*

The religious possibilities of Stoicism were developed further by Epictetus than by any of his Stoic predecessors over the previous 400 years. But his manner of speaking was *not* that of a prissy moralist. He often phrased his pithy remarks in the athletic metaphor: *"Difficulties are what show men's character. Therefore when a difficult crisis meets you, remember that you are as the raw youth, with whom God – the trainer is wrestling."* And in a prayer to God, he uses the military metaphor: *"If Thou sendest me to a place where men have no means of living in accordance with nature, I shall depart this life, not in disobedience to Thee, but as though Thou were sounding for me the recall."* The Stoics accepted suicide, under certain conditions.

And he was funny. Funny, even as he played the part of shock psychologist! He asks and answers the question: *What do you do for friends as you ascend the ladder of intellectual sophistication? Do you hang in with your old pals, or concentrate on intellectual peers?* *"If you do not drink with old friends as you used to drink with them, you cannot be loved by them as much. So choose whether you want to be a boozer and likeable to them, or sober and not likeable."* Then he makes it clear that in his mind, satisfaction and self-respect are best served by escalating friendships apace with your education. *"But if that does not please you, turn about the whole of you, to the opposite; become one of the addicts to unnatural vice, one of the adulterers, and act in corresponding fashion. Yes, and jump up and shout your applause to the dancer!"*

To the painfully shy and reticent student:

*As the good chorus singers do not render solos, but sing perfectly well with a number of other voices, so some men cannot walk around by themselves. Man, if you are anybody, both walk around by yourself, and talk to yourself, and don't hide yourself in the chorus. Let yourself be laughed at sometimes, look about you, shake yourself up, so as to at least find out who you actually are!*

Now neither these eight volumes of Epictetus "lectures," hallway talk, and private conversations, nor their "executive summary," The Enchiridion, were compiled by Epictetus. He couldn't have cared less about being in print. They were taken down in some kind of frantic shorthand by a 23 year-old student, a remarkable man, Flavius Arrianus, usually known as just Arrian. He was an aristocratic Greek born in a Black Sea province of Asia Minor. You can't help but imagine what it took for him to improvise this shorthand and follow the old man around and take down all that material. After getting a load of Epictetus and his "living" speech, he must have said something like: "Wow, we've got to get this guy down on papyrus!" In his dedication of his final manuscript to a friend, he writes: "Whatever I heard him say, I used to write down, word for word, as best I could, endeavoring to preserve it as a memorial, for my own future use, of his way of thinking and the frankness of his speech. Let those who read these words be assured of this: that when Epictetus spoke them, the hearer could not help but feel exactly what Epictetus wanted him to feel." That is the mark of a good teacher!

Arrian was a writer throughout his life. His last and largest book was his definitive text on Alexander the Great's expedition to the east: *The Anabasis of Alexander*. Some time after his death, four of his eight volumes of Epictetus disappeared. During the Middle Ages the four remaining were bound under the title Epictetus's *Discourses*. As I said, *The Enchiridion* was tidbits from all eight volumes, so you'll find things in *The Enchiridion* that are not in *Discourses*.

History gives us snapshots of Arrian's other activities in his illustrious career. After leaving Epictetus's school, and a term as a successful Roman army officer, we find him lecturing in Athens in about 120 A.D., and there meeting Roman Emperor Hadrian, who was about to start a five-year tour of the Empire following his investiture in 117 A.D. Epictetus figured into two fallouts of Arrian's presence in Athens in the years following. Hadrian, in 130 A.D., appointed Arrian consul for a year, followed by six years as governor of the large province of Cappadocia in Asia Minor. Arrian introduced Epictetus to Emperor Hadrian and they became lifetime friends. Secondly, when Arrian vacated his lectureship in Athens for politics, he was relieved by a Q. Janius Rusticus, who later became the tutor to the young Marcus Aurelius. Later, in his book *Meditations*, a book on Stoicism, Emperor Marcus Aurelius acknowledged his debt to Epictetus for the wisdom he gained from studying his eight volumes as a youth. (Rusticus had some copies Arrian left him and gave one to his student, young Aurelius.)

So this slave boy who became a schoolmaster, gained fame as a respected scholar in the highest circles of the only superpower of the ancient world. And those were important years in world history. They are the years the English historian Edward Gibbon was talking about in the famous statement in his book, *The History of the Decline and Fall of the Roman Empire*: "If a man were called upon to fix the period in the history of the world during which the condition of the human race was most happy and prosperous, he would without hesitation name that which elapsed from the accession of Nerva to the death of Marcus Aurelius." That comes to a period of 84 years, from 96 A.D. to 180 A.D. "Their united reigns are possibly the only period in history in which the happiness of a great people was the sole object of government."

The eminent old philosopher Will Durant, in the volume named "Caesar and Christ" in his *History of Civilization* series, calls the five emperors spanning the era that Gibbon admired, "the philosopher kings." All were Stoics or had strong Stoic sympathies: Nerva pardoned exiled Stoics of the Domitian reign. Trajan had a Stoic tutor in his quarters. Hadrian was Epictetus's close friend. Antonius Pius, a "product of the Stoic school," insisted that in Roman law courts, Stoic legal principles be followed, i.e. that (1) in all cases of doubt, judgments be resolved in favor of the accused, and (2) a man should be held innocent until proven guilty. And the last of the philosopher kings, Marcus Aurelius, probably the finest of all Roman Emperors, secretly wrote his Stoic *Meditations* by candlelight in his tent perched on one or another of the mountainsides of Germany, where for the last 12 years of his life he was in the field as Commanding General of the Roman armies, continually engaged in defending the northern frontiers of the Empire against tribal attacks.

The Roman Stoic was more a man of action than contemplation, but listen to the paragraph of old soldier Aurelius on how to die: "Pass this little space of time - your lifetime comfortably, with nature, and end thy journey in contentment, like the ripe olive that falls, praising the earth that gave birth to it, and thanking the tree that made it grow."

On the question of afterlife, Marcus Aurelius took

up and emphasized the teaching of Epictetus. They alone, among Stoics, were very careful in what they said about death. There was no proof of afterlife, and rather than possibly mislead people, they refrained from the more ample language of their predecessors. Matthew Arnold described Marcus Aurelius as "perhaps, the most beautiful figure in history."

The five Stoic philosopher kings were the sort of men you would want to have as Marine Corps Commandants. A few notes from my history books: The second of the five, Trajan, was Commanding General of the Roman army in Cologne when he was notified that Emperor Galba had died, and that *his* number was up. He was Emperor for 19 years, and throughout, habitually wore his army uniform. Tall and robust, he was wont to march on foot with his troops and ford, with full kit, the hundreds of rivers they crossed.

Let me tell you about that five-year trip his successor, Emperor/General Hadrian, took after meeting Arrian in Athens. Accompanied by experts, architects, builders, and engineers, he had left Rome in 121 A.D. to inspect defenses in Germany. He lived the life of his soldiers, eating their fare, never using a vehicle, walking with full military equipment 20 miles at a time. The Roman army was never in better condition than in his reign. He traveled the Rhine to its mouth, sailed to Britain, ordered the building of a wall from Solway Firth to the mouth of the Tyne "to divide the barbarians [Scots] from the Romans [in England]" - "Hadrian's Wall." Back to Gaul, then to Spain, then down into Northwest Africa where he led some garrisoned Roman Legions against Moors who had been raiding the Roman towns of Mauritania. That finished, he boarded one of his Mediterranean warships and went to Ephesus, went up and inspected the ports of the Black Sea, back down to Rhodes, and still curious at 50, stopped in Sicily and climbed Mt. Etna to see the sunrise from a perch 11,000 feet above *his* Mediterranean Sea.

The time interval between my finishing graduate school and becoming a prisoner was almost exactly three years, September 1962 to September 1965. That was a very eventful period in my life. I started a war (led the first-ever American bombing raid on North Vietnam), led good men in about 150 aerial combat missions in flak, and throughout three 7-month cruises to Vietnam I had not only the *Enchiridion*, but the *Discourses* on my bedside table on each of the three aircraft carriers I flew from. And I read them.

On the 9th of September 1965, I flew right into a flak trap, at tree-top level, 500 knots, in a little A-4 airplane-- cockpit walls not even three feet apart - which I couldn't steer after it was on fire, control system shot out. After ejection I had about 30 seconds to make my last statement in freedom before I landed on the main street of that little village right ahead. And so help me, I whispered to myself: "Five years down there at least. I'm leaving the world of technology and entering the world of Epicetus."

I want to step off the chronology escalator for just a minute and explain what memories of the *Enchiridion* and *Discourses* I did have "ready at hand" when I ejected from that plane. What I had in hand was the understanding that the Stoic, particularly the disciple of Epictetus who developed this accounting, always keeps separate files in his mind for: (a) those things which are "up to him" and (b) those things which are "not up to him;" or another way of saying it, (a) those things which are "within his power" and (b) those things which are "beyond his power;" or still another way of saying it: (a) those things which are within the grasp of "his will, his free will," and (b) those things which are beyond it. Among the relatively few things that are "up to me, within my power," within my will, are my opinions, my aims, my aversions, my own grief, my own joy, my moral purpose or will, my attitude toward what is going on, my own good, and my own evil. Please note: All these things, as are all things of real importance to the Stoic, are matters that apply *principally* to your *"inner self,"* where you *live.*

Now I'm talking like a preacher here for a bit. Please understand that I'm not trying to *sell* anything; it's just the most efficient way to explain it. Stoicism is one of those things that, when described analytically, sounds horrible to some modem people. Stoic scholars agree that to describe it effectively, the teacher must "become, for the time being at least," a Stoic.

For instance, to give you a better feel for why "your own good and your own evil" are on the list, I want to quote Alexander Solzhenitsyn from his book *Gulag Archipelago,* when he talks about that point in prison when he gets his act together, realizes his residual powers, and starts what I know as "ascending," riding the updrafts of occasional euphoria as you realize you are getting to know yourself and the world for the first time.

*'It was only when I lay there on the rotting prison straw that I sensed within myself the first stirrings of good. Gradually it was disclosed to me that the line separating good*

*and evil passes not between states nor between social classes nor between political parties, but right through every human heart, through all human hearts. And that is why I turn back to the years of my imprisonment and say, sometimes to the astonishment of those about me, bless you, prison, for having been a part of my life.'*

I *understand* that. He learned, as I and many others have learned, that good and evil are not just abstractions that you kick around and give lectures about, and attribute to this person and that. The only good or evil that mean anything are right in your own heart: within your will, within your power, where it's up to you. What the Stoics say is: "You take care of that, and you'll have your hands full."

What is not up to you? Beyond your power? Not subject to your will in the last instance? For starters, let's take "your station in life." As I glide down toward that little town on my short parachute ride, I'm just about to learn how negligible *is* my control over my station in life. It's not at all up to me. Of course I'm going right now from being the Wing Commander, in charge of a thousand people (pilots, crewmen, maintenance men), responsible for nearly a hundred airplanes, and beneficiary of goodness knows all sorts of symbolic status and goodwill, to being an object of contempt. "Criminal," I'll be known as. But that's not *half* the revelation that is the realization of your *own fragility*, that you can be reduced by the natural elements, or men, to a helpless, sobbing wreck - unable to control even your own bowels - in a matter of minutes. And more than that even, you're going to face fragilities you never before let yourself believe could be true. Like after mere minutes, in a flurry of action while being knocked down and then sat up to be bound with tourniquet-tight ropes, with care, by a professional, hands cuffed behind, jack-knifed forward, head pushed down between your ankles held secure in lugs attached to a heavy iron bar, that with the onrush of anxiety, knowing your upper body blood circulation has been stopped, and feeling the ever growing pain and the ever closing in of claustrophobia as the man standing on your back gives your head one last shove down with his heel and you start to gasp and vomit, that you can be made to blurt out answers, probably correct answers, to questions about anything they know you know. I'm not going to put you through that explanation again. I'll just call it "taking the ropes."

No, any "station in life" can be changed from that of a dignified and competent gentleman of culture to that of a panic-stricken, sobbing, self-loathing wreck, maybe a *permanent* wreck if you have no *will*, in less than an hour. So what? So after you work a lifetime to get yourself all set up, and then delude yourself into thinking that you have some kind of ownership claim on your station in life, you're riding for a fall. You're asking for disappointment. To avoid that, stop kidding yourself, just do the best you can on a common-sense basis to make your station in life what you want it to be, but never get *hooked* on it. Make sure in your heart of hearts, in your inner self, that you treat your station in life with *indifference.* Not with contempt, only with indifference. And so on to a long list of things which some unreflective people assume they're assured of controlling to the last instance - your reputation, for ex- ample. Do what you will, it's at least as fickle as your station in life. *Others* decide what your reputation is. Try to make it as good as possible, but *again*, don't get *hooked* on it. In your heart, when you get out the key and open up that old roll-top desk where you really keep your stuff, don't let "reputation" get mixed up with what's within your *moral purpose*, what's within the power of your *will*, in other words, what's up to *you*. Make sure it's in the bottom drawer, filed under "matters of indifference." And so too with your *health*, your *wealth*, your *pleasure*, your *pain*, your *fame*, your *disrepute*, your *life*, and your *death*. They are all *externals*, all outside your control in the last instance, all outside the power of where you really live. And where you really live is confined to the regime of your moral purpose, confined to matters that can be projected by your acts of will - like desires, aims, aversions, judgments, attitudes, and of course, your good and your evil. For a Stoic, the moral purpose, the will, is the only repository of things of absolute value.

Whether they are projected wisely or foolishly, for good or for evil, is up to you. When his will is set on the right course, a man becomes good; when it's on a foul course, he becomes evil. With the right course comes good luck and happiness, and with the foul course, bad luck and misery. To a Stoic, bad luck is your fault; you've become *addicted* to *externals*.

Epictetus: "What are tragedies, but the portrayal in tragic verse of the sufferings of men who have admired things external?" Not even God will intercede in your decisions. Epictetus: God gives you attributes, like magnanimity, courage, and endurance, to enable you to bear whatever happens. These are given free of all restraint, compulsion, or hindrance; He has put the whole matter under your control without reserving even for Himself any power to prevent or hinder.

As I have said, your deliverance and your destruction are 100 percent *up to you.*

I know the difficulties of gulping all this down right away. You keep thinking of practical problems. Everybody has to play the game of life. You can't just walk around saying: "I don't care about my health, or wealth, or my reputation, or whether I'm sent to prison or not." Epictetus was a great teacher because he could draw a word picture that cleared up the way to look at what he was talking about.

In this case, Epictetus said everybody should play the game of life - that the best play it with "skill, form, speed and grace." But like most games, you play it with a ball. Your team devotes all its energies to getting the ball across the line. But after the game, what do you do with the ball? Nobody much cares. It's not worth anything. The competition, the game, was the thing. You play the game with care, making sure you are never making the external a part of yourself, but merely lavishing your skill in regard to it. The ball was just "used" to make the game possible, so just roll it under the porch and forget it, let it wait for the next game. Most important of all, just don't *covet* it, don't *seek* it, don't *set your heart* on it. It is this latter route that makes externals dangerous, makes them the route to slavery. First you covet or abhor "things," and then along comes he who can confer or remove them. I quote *Enchiridion (The Little Book)* 14: "A man's master is he who is able to confer or remove whatever that man seeks or shuns. Whoever then would be free, let him wish nothing, let him decline nothing, which depends on others, else he must necessarily become a slave." *Discourses* I/121: "Who is your master? He who has authority over any of the things upon which you have set your heart."

These last quotations constitute the real core of what a person needs in order to understand the POW situation.

So I took those core thoughts into prison. I also remembered a lot of attitude shaping remarks from the *Enchiridion 17* on how not to kid yourself into thinking that you can somehow stand aloof, be an "observer of the passing scene," aloof from the prisoner underground organization.

*"Remember that you are an actor in a drama of such sort as the Author chooses: if short, then in a short one; if long, then in a long one. If it be His pleasure that you should enact a poor man, or a cripple, or a ruler, or a private citizen, see that you act it well. For this is your business, to act well the given part. But to choose it belongs to Another."*

The capital A's on Author and Another are Stoic code markings for "another name for God." Our minds are part of the Divine Mind of God; it is like a flame, and individual consciousnesses are sparks in it. Conversely, we are fragments of God; each one of us has within us a part of Him. We're part of God and he's part of us.

Another attitude shaping remark: When in tight straits, you should stifle what's in you of that Student Body President personality, of give-and-take, openness, being responsive, offering counter-options rather than outright refusal to go along. We called people who acted like student body presidents "players" in prison, and tried to prevent them from digging their own graves.

*Enchiridion* 28: *"If a person had delivered up your body to some passer-by, you would certainly be angry. And do you feel no shame in delivering up your own mind to any reviler?"*

All that, over those three years (between graduate school and being shot down), I had put away for the future. Right now, and I'm back on chronology, it's very *quiet* in a parachute, and I can hear the rifle shots down below and can match them up with bullet rips occurring in the parachute canopy above me. Then I can hear the noontime shouting and see the fists waving in the town as my chute hooks a tree but deposits me on a main street in good shape. With two quick-release fastener flips, I'm free of the chute, and immediately gang-tackled by the 10 or 15 town roughnecks I had seen in my peripheral vision, pounding up the street from my right. It felt to me like the quarterback sack of the century. I don't want to make a big thing of this, nor indicate that I was surprised at my reception, but by the time the tackling and pummeling and twisting and wrenching were over, and it lasted for three or more minutes before the guy in the pith helmet got there to blow his whistle, I had a very badly broken leg that I felt sure would be with me for life. And that hunch turned out to be right. And I'll have to say that I felt only minor relief when I hazily recalled crippled Epictetus's admonition in *Enchiridion* 9: *"Lameness is an impediment to the leg, but not to the will; and say this to yourself with regard to everything that happens. For you will find it to be an impediment to something else, but not truly to yourself."*

As an insider, I knew that whole setup on POWs: that the North Vietnamese already held about 30 prisoners in that early September 1965, probably up in Hanoi; that I was the only Wing Commander, Navy or Air Force, to survive an ejection; and that I would be their senior, their

Commanding Officer, and would remain so, very likely, throughout this war, which I felt sure would last at least five years. And here I was starting off crippled and flat on my back.

Well, Epictetus turned out to be right. After a crude operation just to get my knee locked and splayed leg under me, I was on crutches within a couple of months. And the crooked leg, healing itself, was strong enough to hold me up without crutches in a few more. I took command (clandestinely, of course) of the by then 75 pilots due to grow to 466 over the 7½ years - determined "to play well the given part."

I'll drop the prison chronology right there, and concentrate on bringing to light as many more interesting wrinkles of Epictetus and his Stoicism as time will allow.

I would like to say straight off that I have read through and studied the *Discourses*, at least 10 times, to say nothing of my many excursions into the *Enchiridion*, and I have never found a single inconsistency in Epictetus's code of tenets. It is a put together package, free of contradictions. The old boy may or may not appeal to you, but if he turns you off, don't blame it on incoherence; Epictetus has no problem with logic.

I think more needs to be said about good and evil. After all, *the Stoic is indifferent to everything but* good and evil. In Stoic thought, our good and our evil come from the same locus. "Vice and virtue reside in the will alone." "The essence of good and evil lies in an attitude of the will." Solzhenitsyn locates it in the heart, and Epictetus would buy that, or *will*, or *moral purpose*, or *character*, or *soul*, he's not a nitpicker about things like that. What he bears down on is that your good and your evil are the essence of *you*. You *are* moral purpose. You *are* rational will. You are not hair, you are not skin, you are moral purpose - get that beautiful, and you will be beautiful.

That was revealed to Solzhenitsyn when he felt within himself the first stirrings of good. And in that chapter, the old Russian elaborated other truths about good and evil. Not only does the line separating them *not* pass between political or cultural or ethnic groupings, but right through every human heart, through *all* human hearts, he adds that for any individual over the years, this separation line within the heart shifts, oscillates somewhat. That even in hearts *overwhelmed* by evil, one small bridgehead to *good* is retained. And even in the *best* of all hearts, there remains an *un-uprooted* small corner of evil. There is some good and some evil in all of us, and that's Stoic doctrine.

In that same chapter, Solzhenitsyn comments: "If only there were evil people somewhere insidiously committing evil deeds, and it were necessary only to separate them from the rest of us and destroy them. But the line dividing good and evil cuts through the heart of every human being, and who is willing to destroy a piece of his own heart?"

I just want you to know that I connect with that. In a crucible like a torture prison, you reflect, you silently study what makes those about you tick. Once I had taken the measure of my torture guard, watched his eyes as he worked, watched him move, felt him move as he stood on my slumped-over back and cinched up the ropes pulling my shoulders together, I came to know that there was good in him. That was ironic because when he first came in with the new commissar when torture was instigated after I got there, I had nicknamed him "Pigeye" because of the total vacancy of the stare of the one eye he presented as he peeked through cell door peepholes. He was my age, balding and wiry, quick, lithe and strong, like an athletic trainer. He was totally emotionless, thus his emotionless eyes. He had almost no English-language capability, just motions and grunts. Under orders, he put me through the ropes 15 times over the years, and rebroke my bad leg once, I feel sure inadvertently. It was a court martial scene and he was having to give me the ropes before a board of North Vietnamese officers. The officers sat at a long table before Pigeye and me, and behind us was a semi-circle of soldiers bearing rifles with fixed bayonets at a kind of "dangle" position, the bayonet pointing at the cement floor ahead of them. This was in the "knobby" torture room of "New Guy Village" at Hoa Lo prison in August 1967 – so called because the walls had been crudely speckled with blobs of cement the size of an ice cream scoop in a "soundproofing" attempt. I could tell Pigeye was nervous because of these officers whom I had never seen before, and I don't think he had, and he pressed me flat over my bad leg instead of the good one he had always put the tension on before. The healing knee cartilage gave way with a loud "pop," and the officers looked at each other and then got up and left. I couldn't get off that floor and onto my feet for nearly two months.

In all those years, we probably had no more than 24 hours, one-on-one together. But neither of us ever broke the code of an unvaryingly strict "line of duty" relationship. He never tricked me, always played it straight, and I begged no mercy. I admired that in him, and I could tell he did in me. And when people say: "He was a torturer, didn't you *hate* him?" I say, like

Solzehnitsyn, to the astonishment of those about me, "No, he was a good soldier, never overstepped his line of duty."

By that time, I had learned that *fear* and *guilt* are the real pincers that break men's wills. I would chant under my breath as I was marched to interrogation, knowing that I must refuse to comply, and take the ropes: "Your eyes must show no fear; they must show no guilt." The North Vietnamese had learned never to take a prisoner "downtown" - to the payoff for what our whole treatment regime was about - public propaganda exploitation - unless he was truly intimidated, unless they were *sure* he felt *fear*. Their threats had no meaning unless you felt *fear*. They had suffered the political damage of several, including myself, who had acted up, spoken up, and blurted out the truth to the hand-picked audience of foreigners at the press conference. Book IV of *Discourses: "When a man who has set his will neither on dying nor upon living at any cost, comes into the presence of the tyrant, what is there to prevent him from being without fear? Nothing."*

Fear is an *emotion*, and controlling your emotions can be *empowering*.

I think I have mentioned all the things that the Stoics thought were truly "in our power," within the realm of our moral purpose, under the control of our free will, save one category. It requires a little different thinking, so I've saved it for last. I have introduced it already, in part. The Stoics believed that all human *emotions* are acts of will. You're happy because you want to be happy, you're drained or sad when you want to be sad, and fear is *not* something that danger forces on you. When you find yourself afraid, it's time to realize that you decided, wanted, willed that you fear. As I said above, without your having fear, nobody can meaningfully threaten you. In *Discourses*, there is a dialogue something like this, and it was like old home week to me:

When questioned, I had to give him our escape plans; he threatened me with death; I was compelled, I had no choice...That's not right; you had a choice and you made it. It may have been justified, I won't judge that for now. But be honest with yourself. Don't say you had to do *anything* just because you are threatened with death. You simply decided it was better to comply. It was *your will* that compelled you. *Refuse to want to fear and you start acquiring a constancy of character that makes it impossible for another to do you wrong.* Threats have no effect unless you *fear*.

Epictetus says: "Will you then realize that this *epitome* of all the ills that befall man, of his ignoble spirit, of his cowardice, is *not death,* but rather his *fear of death?"*

As I said, learning to take charge of your emotions is *empowering.* When you get there, *Enchiridion* 30 applies: *"No one can harm you without your permission."* And by "harm" Epictetus means, as Stoics always mean, harming your inner self, your self-respect, and your obligation to be faithful. He can break your arm or your leg, but not to worry. They'll heal.

What are some of the guidelines to identifying the good and the evil in Stoic thought?

Well, first, Stoicism goes back to the idea that nature is God's body, and that it doesn't do to try to improve on it. In fact, God and Nature are two aspects of the same thing. God's Soul is the Mind of the universe, and Nature is his body. Just as the Mind is the active, and Nature is the passive, so our minds are active and our bodies passive. Mind over matter; it all happens in your head, so don't worry about your body. The perfect man models himself on this operation of the universe. Nothing is ever lost. All remains in the care of Providence. Just as the universe, in which the Mind of God is imminent and indwelling and moves in a manner self-sufficient and self-ruling, *so the good man is independent, autonomous, a law unto himself, and a follower of the eternal guidance of duty and conscience.*

This is called the coherence of Stoicism, and Cicero used this as the basis of his founding of Natural Law and International Law. *"True law is right reason in agreement with nature."*

The Stoics were good citizens. In politics the Stoic would love his country and hold himself ready to die at any time to avert *its* disgrace *or his own.* But a man's conscience was to be higher than *any* law. A man has a right to be responsible, self-ruling, autonomous.

So on good and evil, where does that leave us? Nothing that is natural can be evil. Death cannot be evil. Disease cannot be evil. Natural disasters cannot be evil. Nothing *inevitable* can be evil. The universe as a whole is perfect, and everything in it has a place in the overall design. Inevitability is produced by the workings of this mechanism. Events do not happen by chance, they arrive by appointment. There is a cause for everything, and "chance" is simply a name for undiscovered causes.

Neither good nor evil can be abstractions. Epictetus said: *"Where do I look for the good and the evil? Within me, in that which is my own."* But for that which is another's *never* employ the words "good" or "evil," or anything of the sort. Goods and evils can *never* be things others *do to you*, or *for you*.

Why not make health or life be good? Because *man deserves the good,* and it's better that he not "deserve" anything he does not control; otherwise, he will go after what is not his, and this is the start of crime, wars, you name it.

Another thing. You do not control God. You must not refer to Him as "good" or "evil." Why not? If you pin these mundane terms on Him, reciting "God is good," people may become tempted, when things God controls run counter to what they're trying to do - weather being unfavorable for farmers or the wind being from the wrong direction for sailors - to start calling Him evil, too. And that's impious. Remember, says Epictetus: *"Piety must be preserved. Unless piety and self-interest be conjoined, piety cannot be maintained in any man."*

Now let me close with some other things that follow from the assumptions of Stoicism that you might not have thought of. The Stoics say that the invincible man is he who cannot be dismayed by any happening outside of his span of control, outside his will, his moral purpose. Does this sound irresponsible to you? Here you have a man who pays no attention as the world blows up around him, so long as he had no part in causing it.

The answer to that depends on whether or not you believe in collective guilt. The Stoics do not. Here is what *The Encyclopedia of Philosophy* says about collective guilt:

'If guilt, in the proper sense, turns on deliberate wrongdoing, it seems that no one can be guilty for the act of another person - there can be no shared or collective or universal guilt. Guilt is incurred by the free choice of the individual....But many have questioned this. Among them are some sociologists who misrepresent in this way the dependence of the individual on society. But the main location of the idea of collective guilt is religion - many forms of doctrines of original sin and universal sin regard guilt as a pervasive state of mankind as a whole.'

Speaking for myself, I think of collective guilt as a manipulative tool. It reminds me of the communist "criticism/self-criticism" technique. Many of the precepts of the Stoics depend on an abhorrence of the concept of collective guilt.

The Stoics believe that every man bears the exclusive responsibility *himself* for his own good and his own evil - and that leads to their further conclusion that *it is impossible to imagine a moral order in which one person does the wrong, and another, the innocent, suffers.* Now add all that to Epictetus's firm belief that we are all born with an *innate* conception of good and evil, and what is noble and what is shameful, what is becoming and unbecoming, what is fitting and inappropriate, what is right to do and what is wrong, and further, remembering that all Stoic talk refers to the inner man, what is going on "way down in here." It follows that the perpetrator of evil pays the full price for his misdeed in suffering the injury of knowing that he has destroyed the good man with him. Man has "moral sense," and he reaps the benefits and pays the price for this inheritance.

This self-knowledge that you have betrayed yourself, destroyed yourself, is the very worst harm that can befall a Stoic. Epictetus says:

- *"No one comes to his fall because of another's deed."*
- *"No one is evil without loss or damage."*
- *"No man can do wrong with impunity."*

I call this whole personal guilt package that Epictetus relied upon, "the reliability of the retribution of the guilty conscience." As I sometimes say, "There can be no such thing as a 'victim;' you can only be a 'victim' of yourself." Remember:

- Controlling your emotions can be empowering.
- Your inner self is what you make it.
- Refuse to want to fear, and you start acquiring a constancy of character that makes it impossible for another to do you wrong.

Somebody asked Epictetus: "What is the fruit of all these doctrines?" He answered with three sharp words:

### *"Tranquility, Fearlessness, and Freedom."*

FOR CONSPICUOUS GALLANTRY

## Sources

**Primary** – Personal conversations between the author and Stockdale in Singapore and California 1980 - 1983.

**Secondary**

Wikipedia articles:[10]
- *Alcatraz Gang*
- *Hanoi March*
- *Hoa Lo Prison*
- *Operation Ivory Coast*
- *James Stockdale*
- *Tap Code*
- *Tonkin Gulf*
- *U.S. POWs During Vietnam War*

Other articles and papers:[11]
- *Our POWs, The Virginian-Pilot*
- *The Prisoner, New York Times*
- *VADM Stockdale Obituary, The Guardian*
- *National Aviation Hall of Fame*
- *Perot's Interim Partner, Seattle Times*
- *The Stockdale Legacy, SD Union-Tribune*
- *The Stockdale Paradox*
- *Sybil Stockdale, POW Wife Dies, SD Union-Tribune*
- *Stockdale on Stoicism: Master of My Fate*
- *Stockdale on Stoicism: The Stoic Warrior's Triad*

**Images**[12]

---

[10] See online articles for detail regarding sources and references.
[11] See Chapter footnotes.
[12] Cover, pages 12-19, page 81 – Wikimedia Commons

REMEMBERING JAMES STOCKDALE

# The Author

JIM REDMAN was the CEO of a diversified San Diego based industrial firm that was a prime contractor to the U.S. Navy. He first met Admiral Stockdale in Singapore and was privileged to know him personally during the early 1980s.

Jim is a life member of the U.S. Navy League and author of several books, including *The World According to Max*, *Searching for Jacob Waltz*, and *Timeless Quotes, Quips and Wise Sayings*.

FOR CONSPICUOUS GALLANTRY

Made in the USA
Columbia, SC
28 May 2020